Tips and Tricks to Dog Training

A How-To Set of Tips and Techniques for Different Species of Dogs: Based on Real Experiences and Cases

Paul Davis

© Copyright 2019 - All rights reserved.

The content contained within this book may not be reproduced, duplicated or transmitted without direct written permission from the author or the publisher.
Under no circumstances will any blame or legal responsibility be held against the publisher, or author, for any damages, reparation, or monetary loss due to the information contained within this book, either directly or indirectly.
Legal Notice:
This book is copyright protected. It is only for personal use. You cannot amend, distribute, sell, use, quote or paraphrase any part, or the content within this book, without the consent of the author or publisher.
Disclaimer Notice:
Please note the information contained within this document is for educational and entertainment purposes only. All effort has been executed to present accurate, up to date, reliable, complete information. No warranties of any kind are declared or implied. Readers acknowledge that the author is not engaging in the rendering of legal, financial, medical or professional advice. The content within this book has been derived from various sources. Please consult a licensed professional before attempting any techniques outlined in this book.
By reading this document, the reader agrees that under no circumstances is the author responsible for any losses, direct or indirect, that are incurred as a result of the use of information contained within this document, including, but not limited to, errors, omissions, or inaccuracies.

Table of Contents

INTRODUCTION 1

CHAPTER 1
THE BASICS 3

   WHAT TO KNOW BEFORE TRAINING 3
      Put Thought Into the Name 4
      Have One Consistent Way to Grab Your Dog's Attention 4
      Consistency Is Key 5
      Patience Is Another Key 5
      Prepare for Your Dog to Come Home 5
      Don't Push Aside the Crate 7
      Think About Your Training and Discipline 8
   COMMON DOG TRAINING METHODS 10
      Positive Reinforcement Training 10
      E-collar Training 11
      Relationship-based Training 13
      Dominance Training 16

CHAPTER 2
TRAINING AND YOUR DOG 18

   DOG BREEDS AND TRAINING 18
      Border Collie 18
      German Shepherd 19
      Doberman Pinscher 20
      The Pembroke Welsh Corgi 20
      Norwich Terrier 21
      Labrador Retriever 21
      What Makes a Dog Easily Trainable? 22
   CARING FOR YOUR DOG 23
      Choose the Best Food 23
      Keep a Clean Living Environment 24
      Veterinarian Check-ups Are Important 24
      Keep Your Dog's Mouth Clean 25
      Perform Weekly Health Checks Yourself 25
   TIPS TO OVERCOME TRAINING CHALLENGES 25
      Teaching Your Dog Their Name 26
      Pulling on Their Leash 26
      Obedience School 28

    Find a Trusted Personal Trainer 29
  DIFFERENT WAYS TO REWARD YOUR DOG 29
    Play a Game for a Few Minutes 30
    Take a Trip to a Dog Park 30
    Give Them Attention 30
  PREPARING YOUR DOG FOR TRAINING 31
    Prepare Any Documents 31
    Bring Your Dog for a Check-up 31
    Understand Your Dog's Attention Span 32
    Make Sure Your Dog's Stomach is Empty 32
    Have Everything Ready for the Training Session 32
  KEYS FOR SUCCESSFUL DOG TRAINING 33

CHAPTER 3
TIPS AND TRICKS FOR TRAINING YOUR PUPPY 35

  KNOW YOUR PUPPY BEFORE TRAINING BEGINS 35
  TIPS FOR TRAINING YOUR PUPPY 37
    Have Patience 37
    Your Puppy Is at the In-Between Stage 37
    Your Puppy Has Fears 38
    Understand Your Puppy's Developmental Stages 39
  FOUNDATION TRAINING 43
    Potty Training 43
    Bed Training 44
    Home Base Training 45

CHAPTER 4
TIPS AND TRICKS FOR TRAINING YOUR ADOLESCENT DOG 50

  WHAT YOU NEED TO KNOW ABOUT YOUR ADOLESCENT DOG 50
    Teething Is Almost Over! 51
    Bond, Then Bond Some More 51
    Keep Your Dog Social 51
    Your Dog Is Not Going to Sleep As Much 52
    Did the Previous Training Fade Away? 52
    Previous Dog Training? 53
  BASIC TRAINING 53
    Come Training 54
    Lay Down Training 54
    Stay Training 57
    Get Down Training 59
  REAL LIFE TRAINING 60
    What to Do With Aggressive Dogs? 61
  BEYOND BASIC TRAINING 62
    Pulling on the Leash 62
    A Digging Dog 64
    Tug and Release 65

    Teaching Your Dog to Play Fetch 66
    Peekaboo 68
    Boing 69
    Time Out 70
    Roll Over 71
    Hunting 72

CHAPTER 5
TIPS AND TRICKS FOR TRAINING YOUR ADULT DOG 74

  KEEPING YOUR ADULT DOG HEALTHY 75
    Make Sure You Are Feeding Your Dog the Right Food 75
    Include Healthy Activities Into Your Dog's Schedule 75
    Track Your Dog's Weight 76
    Increase Your Visits to the Veterinarian's Office 76
  ADULT DOG TRAINING TECHNIQUES 76
    Training Tips for Older Dogs 77
    Back Up 78
    Stand on a Platform 81
    Touching a Target 83
    Cleaning Up Toys 85
    Catch a Ball 86

CHAPTER 6
TIPS AND TRICKS FOR TRAINING YOUR SENIOR DOG 88

  KEEPING A SENIOR DOG HEALTHY 89
    Pay Close Attention to Their Diet 89
    Dental Hygiene 89
    Make Sure Your Dog Gets Exercise 90
    Provide Your Dog with Special Accommodations 90
  TRAINING TECHNIQUES FOR SENIOR DOGS 90
    Training Tips for Senior Dogs 91
    Which Hand? 92

CHAPTER 7
SO, YOU WANT TO TRAIN YOUR DOG TO DANCE AND OTHER TRICKS 96

  KEEPING YOUR DOG ACTIVE 96
  ALWAYS REMEMBER SAFETY 97
  TRADITIONAL FAVORITES 98
    Sit Pretty 98
    Speak 99
    Shake Hands 100
  SILLY DOG TRICKS 101
    Act Ashamed 101
  EXPERT TRICKS 102
    Find the Car Keys or Remote 102

    Get the Mail *103*
  D ANCING 104
    Heel Forward and Backward *104*
    Take a Bow *105*

CHAPTER 8
COMMON MISTAKES 106

  Mistake #1: Training Your Dog for Too Long *106*
  Mistake #2: You Lack Consistency *107*
  Mistake #3: You Wait Too Long to Start Training *108*
  Mistake #4: You Use Harsh Discipline *109*
  Mistake #5: You Stop Training *109*
  Mistake #6: You Don't Train in the Right Mindset *109*
  Mistake #7: Abusing the Training Tools *110*

CONCLUSION 111
REFERENCES 115

Introduction

You are sitting on your couch watching your new puppy run around the house. They only came home a few hours ago and already into everything. As you watch your dog run from one side of the room to the next, you can't help but smile and wonder what you got yourself into. Can you handle a puppy? Of course, you can! You can handle training any dog with the tips and tricks laid out in this book.

Like with every new topic, you have to start with the basics. You will find this information in Chapter 1. You will receive information on what you need to know before training and common training methods. You will gain an idea of if you are interested in the electric collar, relationship-based training, or positive reinforcement training. It is important to note immediately that every type of training focuses on positive reinforcement at the end of the training step or session.

Chapter 2 gives you more information about training and your dog. There are dog breeds that are easier to train and some that are more stubborn. The type of breed you get does matter when it comes to training. For example, if you want to train a dog specifically for hunting, you will want to look into a dog whose main instinct is to hunt. These dogs, such as Labrador Retrievers, are the easiest dogs to train for hunting. While Poodles are great dogs for training, they are not the best dogs to train for hunting. However, they are great dogs for agility training.

Another part of training your dog is to make sure you are caring for your dog correctly. You will want to keep in mind that they need a certain diet, especially if they are agility training. You will also receive tips about keeping your dog's mouth clean and performing weekly health check-ups, which is especially important for your older dogs.

And what about those training challenges? Every dog, no matter how easy they are to train, is going to come with their own training challenges. How do you help your dog overcome these challenges? You will learn about this within the pages of this book.

Chapters 3, 4, 5, and 6, focus on training dogs at different ages. For example, Chapter 3 looks at training puppies and mainly focuses on the basic training, such as sitting, because dogs are only puppies for a short period of time, and they don't receive a lot of training time. Chapter 4 looks at training dogs during their adolescent phase and continues with basic training. Chapter 5 goes into training an adult dog and Chapter 6 looks at training a senior dog. Each of these chapters also hold training tips and other great information to help you and your dog through the training journey.

Chapter 8 is here to help you understand some of the common mistakes dog owners make throughout the training process. These mistakes each have ideas to help you overcome the mistakes. The key to making sure you don't fall victim to some of the common mistakes is to remain mindful of your training. For example, if you are going to use the electric collar to train your dog, you want to have the remote with you whenever the e-collar is on your dog. By remaining mindful, you will realize when you don't have the remote with you and find it before you need it to train your dog not to dig in the garbage.

Now, it's time to take a deep breath, realize you and your dog will make a great team for training, and focus on the tricks and tips within this book. While you do not receive all the tricks that your dog can learn (there are hundreds of tricks) you will get a variety of tricks to keep any level of dog at any age happy and healthy.

Chapter 1

The Basics

Training your dog can make you feel overwhelmed, it doesn't matter if you are focusing on basic training, such as sitting and laying down, or advanced techniques, such as dog sports. There are moments you will become frustrated, no matter how patient and calm you feel. Then, there are those wonderful moments—the times your dog succeeds at a new trick. It's these moments where you feel that all your hard work has paid off.
But why do people focus on the end result when they are training? Professional trainers will tell you that you have to celebrate every moment your dog made an effort with their training, even if they made a mistake.
Celebrating the missteps your dog takes during training won't make them put in less effort. It won't tell them that this moment is "good enough." It will tell them that you are proud of them for trying. You're proud of them for working hard and you want to reward them with positive reinforcement. Doing this will get your dog focused on the task and want to make you happy again.
Celebrating the moments with positive reinforcement, even when a mistake is made, is one of the first points you need to understand when it comes to training.

What to Know Before Training

Celebrating is not the only point you need to understand before you start training. You need to understand that your dog's personality depends on how well they will train. You need to know about training tools, how your dog's age matters, and how your mindset matters.

Put Thought Into the Name

Naturally, you will choose a name that you love, but if you know you'll spend a lot of time training your new family member, it's important to think of a name that will catch your dog's attention. Names with strong consonants that are short work great. They will perk up your dog's ears, making it easier for you to catch their attention. Some great names to consider are Ginger, Jack, and Jasper. You may think you can only give your little eight-week-old puppy a name and not your older dog you received from the shelter. It's important to know the name of your dog from the shelter tends to be temporary. While this isn't always the case, most shelters don't know the dog's name when they receive them. Call your dog by their shelter name and notice their reaction. If they don't respond, they don't know that you are calling them, and you can rename your dog. Even if you have a dog that responds to a name, you can still change it. This can give you a good start on learning how to train your dog.

Have One Consistent Way to Grab Your Dog's Attention

Dogs are easily distracted by their environment, especially puppies. This causes problems with training because their owners feel they aren't listening to them. In reality, your dog became distracted and didn't know you were talking to them. By setting up a way to grab your dog's attention, such as calling their name, you will train them to look at you.

For example, you notice your dog is in the yard sniffing something on the ground, but they are too close to the road. Because the way you get your dog's attention is to snap your fingers, you head outside and snap your fingers twice. Even though you are several feet from your dog, they are used to this sound and know you are calling to them. They look up and listen to your command to "come."

Consistency Is Key

One of the strongest ways to effectively train your dog is remaining consistent. It is always possible you won't catch your dog in action or be unable to reach your dog when they misbehave, meaning you have to let this one slide as they won't understand what they did wrong. When it comes to these moments, you need to realize they happen. The trick is to not let them happen often. Professional trainers say you have about five seconds to correct your dog's behavior. Once this time passes, you need to let it go and try to catch them in the act the next time.

Patience Is Another Key

Another strong key feature when it comes to training is patience. If you have expectations that your dog will learn to sit by the end of the day, you must lower your expectations. It will take days to weeks to train your dog one trick and you will never stop training.
You will need more patience for a dog you just brought home as it takes them time to adjust to their new environment and for an older dog. Senior dogs are slower than puppies. They aren't going to catch on to new tricks as quickly and can show more stubbornness because they are used to their ways. However, with patience, consistency, and positive reinforcement you will teach your old dog new tricks.

Prepare for Your Dog to Come Home

Just as people prepare to bring their baby home, you want to prepare to bring your dog home. This doesn't mean you need to set up a whole room, but make a spot for their bed, crate, food, water, and some toys. Your dog needs their space just like you need your space. It'll help them feel more at ease and comfortable in their new environment. Plus, they will immediately start to feel that you care.

You hear about dogs sleeping in bed with their companions, but this isn't the idea you want to give a dog you're training. Teach them everyone sleeps in their own space. If possible, give your dog space that isn't around other people or pets. It's common for people with more than one dog to set up their kennels or beds right next to each other. If your dogs laying next to each other brings comfort to them, it's fine to allow it. But, make sure that both your dogs understand they each have a bed and space. There will be times they want to be alone.

Other ways to prepare for your dog to come home:

- Plan the arrival: If you work during the day, try to bring your dog home on a Friday night or Saturday morning. Spend the weekend getting to know your dog by taking them around their new environment, observing their behavior, and playing with them. Give them as much love and support as possible because they are frightened and uneasy about their new home. They need to trust you before they can truly enjoy their new surroundings.

- Gather any supplies you will need: At first you may think your dog needs a couple of dishes for water and food, a bed, crate, and a few toys. However, there are a lot of other supplies you can bring into your dog's environment immediately to help them prepare for training from the start. For example, a leash, collar, and any other training tools you will choose.

    Also, a couple of old towels or rugs are a good idea for several reasons. It can give your dog's space a more comfortable look and be quickly available in case your dog has any accidents. Even a potty-trained dog can have accidents when they first come to a new house.

- Think about your other pets: Animals are sensitive, and they will get jealous of the new family member if you don't give them enough attention. It's common to tell ourselves our other pets "will adjust" and we "don't need to worry." The truth is, you should worry about how all your pets feel. Try to play with all of your pets, make sure you give everyone equal attention, and talk to them when they walk by. Animals love to hear your voice and it makes them feel comfortable.

- Make sure everyone is healthy: Even if you are told the shelter gave your dog a check-up, bring them into the veterinarian's office as soon as possible. Not only can you ensure your dog is healthy, but your vet and dog can start their friendship. You should also take your other pets in for a check-up, especially if it's been a few months or more. It's always a good idea to make sure everyone is healthy for the new arrival. Unless you are going to breed, think spaying or neutering your dog if they aren't already. The veterinarian will guide you through this process.

Don't Push Aside the Crate

It's easy for you to see a crate as a jail cell for a dog, but dogs see a crate as a place to call their own. As long as you don't make your dog stay in the crate most of the day, you will find your dog lounging in their crate at times.
One factor to consider with a crate is how you will use it. If you want to use the crate as a way to punish your dog for bad behavior, you won't want them sleeping in the crate. In this case, you will want to think about getting a bed and a crate or two different types of crates. You don't want to tell your dog to go to bed in the same crate you give them a time out in because they can confuse the two meanings. If your dog feels you are angry with them during the night, they aren't going to sleep well, causing them to become sick or depressed.

Think About Your Training and Discipline

Some people use training as a way to combat disciplining their dog. They believe training their dog to listen to their commands and using a firm voice is all they need. For most dogs, this will work as long as you are training your dog correctly and consistently. Even if this is the way you want to go, it is helpful to look into the best ways to use any form of discipline. You also need to be aware that certain forms of discipline will have serious consequences.

Correctly disciplining your dog is not an easy task. It will take planning and ensuring that every family member is on the same page. This is something you will also need to do with training. To effectively discipline your dog, consider the following tips:

- Your dog shouldn't know that you are disciplining them. If your dog realizes it is you, they will misbehave when you aren't around. This is one reason why a lot of people turn to training in order to teach their dog how to behave.

- Your dog lives in the moment. If you discipline your dog a minute after the unwanted behavior, they will associate the discipline with their current action and not their previous action.

- Do not use discipline with an aggressive dog. This can make their aggression worse. If you find yourself struggling with an aggressive dog, it's time to think about obedience classes or a professional trainer who can help you.

- You need to teach your dog a wanted behavior to replace the unwanted behavior. This is another reason people like to use training. However, you should never think of training as a form of discipline.

- Don't severely discipline your dog for a small crime and don't weakly discipline them for a big crime. This is a difficult imaginary line to find, but it is necessary. Think of it this way: If you are too harsh on your dog, you're going to make them frightened and weaken any trust and respect within your relationship. If your discipline is weak, it won't cause the dog to work on changing their behavior.

There are many ways that you should never discipline your dog because it will cause problems in the future.

- You should never hit your dog, not even a pat on the nose. Dogs are highly sensitive animals and this action will cause them to trauma, especially if it happens continuously.

- Never knee or kick your dog. You can easily hurt them, and it will cause them trauma.

- Don't "rub your dog's nose in it." If your dog has an accident, look over your training procedure or take your dog to the veterinarian to ensure it's not a medical issue.

- Don't yell at your dog. This is often our automatic reaction when they run into the street or do something that's unsafe. Yelling is similar to hitting or kicking with a dog, as it can easily traumatize them.

- Don't jerk the leash when your dog pulls you on a walk. Take time to train your dog so they don't take part in this behavior.

Common Dog Training Methods

There are many methods you can use to train your dog. In fact, you may find yourself overwhelmed by all the methods and struggle finding the best one for you and your dog. You might find yourself using one method, but not liking it after a while because you don't feel like your dog is responding to the method. While it is likely your dog needs a different method, it's important that you analyze your training method before changing on your dog.
There is a lot of disagreement with the various methods I discuss in this section. For example, many people won't use the e-collar because they think the shock will harm their dog. While it can, if you use the e-collar correctly your dog will barely notice the shock and still respond by stopping the behavior.

Positive Reinforcement Training

You always want to give your dog positive reinforcement when they do something well. Therefore, this type of training should be a part of any other form of training. However, it can also stand alone. This type of training has been around for a long period of time, but it's gained popularity over the last few years.
When you focus on positive reinforcement training, you are constantly giving your dog rave reviews when they show good behavior. The main idea behind this training method is that dogs will naturally repeat behavior when they receive positive reinforcement. As long as you remain consistent with the positive reinforcement, your dog will follow the behavior that gives them the attention they desire.
When a dog exhibits unwanted behavior, you simply don't respond. You don't talk to them, you don't pet them, and you don't give them any type of positive reinforcement. This is one of the biggest problems people have when using positive reinforcement. They don't understand how you can ignore your dog's bad behavior and it will go away.

It is important to note that the more stubborn breeds will have a harder time learning through this method because they are more likely to continue their negative behavior. While they love positive reinforcement as much as an easily trainable dog breed, they won't care that you are ignoring certain behavior. Instead, they will see this as an open window to continue the behavior. Dogs that are easily trainable and more sensitive will notice you don't pay attention when they perform certain actions and more than likely stop the behavior or at least decrease it.

Using positive reinforcement training means you have to be on your toes with your dog at all times. You will need to supervise them well to give them positive reinforcement within seconds of their good behavior. If you don't catch them soon enough, they won't understand why they are receiving the extra attention from you and will associate it with the behavior they exhibited at the time.

When you start rewarding behavior for training, you will give them positive reinforcement every time they exhibit the behavior. After they catch on to the training and their behavior becomes more regular and natural, you will start giving them positive reinforcement every other time, then every third time, etc. You want to gradually decrease the positive reinforcement you give with that behavior. This is another piece people struggle with during positive reinforcement training. People want to give their dog attention all the time, but they can't when using this form of training.

E-collar Training

The e-collar is known as the electrical collar and delivers signals, such as a tone, vibration, and shock to your dog's neck. It's important to realize the e-collar is not meant to be a way to discipline your dog. Unfortunately, there are people who use their e-collar for this purpose. They will give their dog a shock every time they do something wrong. The e-collar is meant to be a teaching tool, one that trains your dog to stop the unwanted behavior without realizing it is you giving them the shock. Instead, they believe their behavior caused the shock, making them stop the behavior over a period of time.

There are various types of e-collars and you need to choose the one that is right for your dog. For example, if you are training your dog to hunt, you will purchase a hunting e-collar. For focusing on house training, you will purchase a yard e-collar. You need to look at the basics of the e-collar because each one is a bit different. For instance, a yard e-collar ranges to ½ to ¾ of a mile. This means you can send signals to your dog with the remote until they pass this point. The furthest e-collars tend to go is about a mile. These are typically the e-collars used for hunting.

If you choose to use the e-collar, you want your dog to become used to the device before you start using it. It is advised that you let your dog wear it for a week before you turn it on and start training. You want to train during this time as the e-collar is not necessary for early training. When you start using the e-collar, set it on its lowest stimulation level. If your dog reacts by turning their neck a bit, they can feel the shock and you shouldn't increase the stimulation level. Most dogs will feel the shock at the lowest setting.

Do not use e-collars on dogs younger than five to six months old. While some smaller e-collars will fit on them, most people feel the training is still in its early stages where it is best to use verbal cues and hand gestures to train your dog.

Case Example: Tallie's Garbage Training

Tallie is a Border Collie who loved to go through the garbage inside and outside of the home. After trying to get Tallie to stay out of the garbage for months using their regular training method, they decided to get an e-collar. When the e-collar arrived, Tallie's owners read the instruction manual. They placed the e-collar closer to the top of Tallie's neck so it wouldn't slip when she was playing. After making sure the collar was not too tight by placing two fingers between her neck and the e-collar, the couple allowed Tallie to get used to her e-collar for a week. They kept the e-collar off and never used it to train her to stay out of the garbage. Instead, they continued to use their regular method.

After the week passed, Tallie's owners turned her e-collar on and waited until they found her in the garbage to send any signals. Through their research on e-collars, Tallie's owners understood they had to send the signal at the right moment, or the training would have poor consequences. Therefore, Tallie didn't receive her shock until her nose was in the garbage. Her owners worried if they shocked her walking up to the garbage, she would become afraid of garbage cans and be uncomfortable in certain areas of their home.

When Tallie received the shock, she moved her head to the side a bit, got down from the garbage, and shook her head. At the lowest stimulation setting, Tallie's owners knew that she felt the shock, so they did not need to raise the stimulation level.

Tallie's e-collar stayed on her neck during the day. When she went to bed, her owners placed a dummy collar on her neck to give her the impression it is the same collar. In the morning, Tallie's owners replaced the dummy collar with the e-collar and continued focusing on her garbage training. Within a few days, Tallie started to hesitate when she got close to the garbage. Sometimes she would go the other way and sometimes she jumped into the garbage and started digging until she received a shock. Within a couple of weeks, Tallie stopped getting into the garbage.

Relationship-based Training

Relationship-based training is a new type of training that takes a lot of observation as it focuses on your dog's body language. You train your dog by the way they react, so you can get a better understanding of the way they think and establish stronger communication. Many people refer to this type of training a philosophy in dog training. You can use this type of training for changing old behaviors and forming new behaviors. You do this by reinforcing the behavior you want to see. This type of training works because dogs strive on making sure their owners are happy.

Relationship-based training informs people that every interaction you have with your dog is a teachable moment. You need to become mindful, so you are aware of the way you are acting and treating your dog, other people, other animals, and yourself. Your dog notices everything from your actions to your emotions. Dogs have a very strong sense when it comes to their owner's emotions. They can tell how their owners are feeling and can quickly sense when something is not right.

Here are a few tips for relationship-based training:

- Place your animal's immediate needs first: If you find that your dog is acting uneasy, fearful, or looking for a place to hide you need to cease training. It is more important that you try to understand why your dog is reacting this way. They are telling you that something is wrong and one of their immediate needs is not being met. It is important to solve this problem before continuing with training.

- Learn what motivates your dog: Observing your dog's behavior and how they react to stimuli will help you realize what motivates your dog. For example, you are training your dog to sit down every time you say the word "sit." Each time your dog sits when given the command, you praise your dog by playing with them and telling them how proud you are and what a good dog they are. Even if they don't understand every word you say, the tone of your voice and your actions inform your dog that you are happy with their behavior. They will remember this and the next time they hear the word "sit" they will follow the action that gave them praise.

One time, you decide to change your method with training a little. Instead of giving your dog praise, you give them a treat. Every time you tell them to "lay down" and they listen, you toss a treat at them. Over time, you notice that your dog reacts stronger to the praise than the treat. When praising them, your dog catches on to the training quicker. Therefore, you continue to use praise when training your dog instead of giving them a treat.

- Learn how to interpret your dog's body language: Every dog will show signs of how they are feeling, such as sadness, anger, and fear. Unfortunately, there are a lot of myths surrounding the ways to read your dog's body language. Receiving the wrong information will cause you to misinterpret how your dog is feeling, breaking down a trusting and respectful relationship.

When you decide to train through the relationship-based method, you have to do your research to understand how your dog's breed reacts when they are feeling a certain way. Try to stick to the scientific based information and talk to professionals. You can start with a dog trainer as they can help you or guide you to the right information and people to talk to.

- Change your dog's environment to prevent their unwanted behavior: This idea is similar to "child proofing," but you "dog proof" your dog's environment to prevent them from acting a certain way. For example, your dog likes to get into the garbage located in their space, so you take the garbage out. The other garbage bins your dog gets into should have lids and be shut in cupboards or closets, giving your dog limited access to these areas.

- Supervise your dog carefully: Don't allow your dog to run around the whole house without supervision, especially if they get into everything or are not potty trained. Keep them with you as much as possible and follow them around the house if they start to wander. You don't have to do this for your dog's whole life. Once they go beyond the basic training level, you will decrease supervision. The point is to keep a close eye on your dog until they have the necessary life skills to know when they need to grab your attention to go outside or to stay out of the garbage.

Like other forms of training, you need to be realistic with training. This will help you overcome any obstacles because you will have lower expectations for how quickly your dog will catch on to training or how often your dog will listen to your commands. No matter how well you train your dog, you will feel there are moments they have selective hearing.

Dominance Training

Dominance training is also known as alpha dog training. This type of training focuses on the instinctual pack mentality of dogs. While your dog isn't around a pack of dogs, they see the family unit as a pack. With this knowledge, the owner can become the alpha, causing the dog to listen to what they say and do. This is another training method where you use your dog's body language to learn how they are feeling.

When you focus on this training, you will want to make sure your dog sees you go first, as the alpha always goes first. For example, you will leave the room first, enter the room first, and receive your food first. You will even walk before them when they are on the leash. If your dog wants to go outside, they have to sit by the door quietly until you let them go outside.

Dominance training is hard for some people because you need to make your dog feel they are underneath you. For instance, when your dog is afraid, one of the best techniques to calm your furry friend is to get down to their level. When you use dominance training, you can't get down to your dog's level, no matter how they feel. You always need to tower over your dog to assert your authority.

Dominance training is starting to decline in the modern world. New studies are coming out to show that dogs don't follow the pack mentality like wolves, making this training ineffective (Clark, n.d.). Professional dog trainers don't usually agree with this training because they feel it is out of date. Most trainers like to follow the scientific studies on how dogs react to training as this gives them better results.

Chapter 2

Training and Your Dog

One of the biggest factors to determine how well training will go with your dog depends on their personality. Your dog's personality depends on the way your treat them and their breed. There are some breeds that are easily trainable and other breeds that harder to train. However, every dog can learn tricks. The key is how you handle the training.

Dog Breeds and Training

It is important to note that all dogs enjoy pleasing their owner and this factor helps when it comes to training. No matter what dog breed you have, you can use this knowledge to help train your dog. If you are looking for an easier time when training, you will want to focus on the easily trainable dogs.

Border Collie

The Border Collie is a smart, energetic, and affectionate dog. They thrive on positive reinforcement, so are a strong candidate for this type of training. They are sensitive dogs and want to do anything they can to make sure their owners are happy. They generally have a height of 18 to 22 inches, so they are great dogs for any type of living. But if you live in a smaller apartment you need to make sure your dog gets enough exercise. You can do this by bringing your dog outside often and taking them to obedience classes.

Border Collies are great dogs for agility training. They love to perform tricks and play in dog sports. They are great show dogs, as long as they are healthy and well cared for. They are in the herding dog family, making them feel they need to herd children in a large group.

Border Collies have more energy than people realize. They are fast runners and quick to catch on to what you are teaching them. They will amaze you with how much they can handle in a day. Many people who train Border Collies say they will finish a task and then look at you as if they want a new task. They don't tire easily, making them one of the best dogs for training.

German Shepherd

The German Shepherd is often used for training for police and military work. They are great dogs to train due to their courageous, confident, and smart nature. Because they are large dogs, reaching anywhere from 22 to 26 inches, they are best in a bigger home. They can adapt to apartment living but will need a lot of time to run around and exercise.

One of the reasons the German Shepherd makes the list of easily trainable dogs is because they are extremely loyal. Once they understand the behavior they are supposed to exhibit, they will do their best to follow this behavior. Furthermore, they can focus on tasks easily and have the ability to learn several tasks in a short period of time.

Unlike some breeds, German Shepherds can focus longer on tasks, allowing you to train them for a longer period of time. Of course, you always need to take your dog's age into consideration. Puppies are going to naturally need more breaks than older dogs, even German Shepherds.

It is important to know when your dog is becoming tired because they won't tell you they need a break. They will keep going until you give them a break. When you feel your German Shepherd needs a break, it is best to stop training and allow them to rest.

German Shepherds have a keen sense of danger and have no trouble putting their life on the line to save the people they love. They don't become scared easily, so they can handle most types of consistent training.

Doberman Pinscher

Doberman Pinschers are loyal, and fearless. They aren't afraid to take on new challenges and are great dogs for a source of protection. Due to their larger size, reaching anywhere from 24 to 28 inches at the shoulder, apartment living isn't the greatest for them. But, with enough time to run and exercise outside, they will adjust.

One cautionary tale is many people believed only experienced trainers should focus on Doberman Pinschers. While they are easy to train, consistency is more important for this breed. They do get distracted easier than other breeds because of their protective nature. They will notice every single noise coming from their environment and keep their eye in this area until they know everything is fine.

Another reason is because Dobermans are known for their aggressive nature. In reality, any breed will become aggressive under certain circumstances. The way you treat your dog will shape their aggressive natures, especially if you get them as a puppy. Dog's learn through how and what they are taught. If you are aggressive with your dog, even in play, they will become more aggressive. This is why it is always important to talk to your dog calmly and never react in an aggressive way toward your dog.

The Pembroke Welsh Corgi

The Pembroke is a smaller dog that can live in any type of environment. They love the apartment life as well as the country life. However, they also need a lot of room to explore or they will become bored, which can lead to depression in dogs.

The Pembroke needs to have a job to complete to stay happy. Even if you aren't training them at the time, it is important you play and interact with them often to give them a sense that they are doing their job. The Pembroke is part of the herding dog family and will try to herd people. However, with the right consistent training you can teach them when and when not to herd.

The Pembroke is a great dog if you are interested in agility training because of their enthusiastic nature. While they are easily trainable, you always need to make sure you have the role of boss. Pembrokes feel they have to be the boss and won't have any trouble trying to take that title away from you.

Norwich Terrier

The Norwich Terrier is a smaller dog that is suitable for any type of living situation. They are great with children and are energetic, even when they feel tired. It is easy to get a Norwich Terrier to jump up and complete a task, but it is also important to not overwork your dog when training. Norwich Terriers will allow you to do this because they strive to make their owners happy. Therefore, it is often up to you to watch for signs to note that your little companion needs a break.

They are intelligent dogs and make for a great breed to train for dog sports. They not only need physical exercise, but also mental exercise. In fact, they won't be truly happy unless you challenge them physically and mentally. Even though the Norwich Terrier is small in size, they are great hunting dogs.

Labrador Retriever

Labrador Retrievers are friendly, outgoing, and active, making them easily trainable. As larger dogs, reaching between 21 to 24 inches at the shoulder, they are more comfortable in a larger space. However, they can adapt to apartment life. Just as any other medium to large sized dog, you need to make sure to take them out for enough exercise. In fact, these dogs love to see how far they can go.

The Labrador Retriever is a great dog for any type of training. They are natural hunters, making them easy to train for hunting. Furthermore, they enjoy taking part in dog sports and shine in agility training. They are sociable dogs and enjoy spending time with humans and other animals.

What Makes a Dog Easily Trainable?

There are dozens of dog breeds that are considered easily trainable. If you want to focus on a dog that is known to train easily, here are some factors to consider:

- What drives your dog's instincts? Each breed has their own instinct triggers. Some of these triggers are stronger for your dog than others. When your dog is faced with stronger triggers, they will have a harder time focusing. For example, if a dog is ruled by their nose, they will have a harder time concentrating on a task if they smell something new in their environment. They will feel the need to learn what this new smell is before they can learn how to sit.

- Is your dog easily distracted? Puppies are naturally more distracted by features in their environment than older dogs. But there are also many breeds that have to focus on a new sound they heard or what they saw moving.

- Your dog's personality. One of the biggest features when looking for an easily trainable dog is to do a little background research on your dog's personality. There are dogs that will cooperate better than other breeds and some that will try to take over control. Of course, the dogs that are known to cooperate will give you an easier training time.

Caring for Your Dog

Most of these tips you will want to follow whether training your dog or not. It is important to make sure your dog is fit, healthy, and happy. When focusing on a healthy and happy dog, there are ten components that you need to follow:
1. Security and safety
2. Nutrition
3. Love
4. Exercise
5. Veterinary care
6. Grooming
7. Comfortable place to sleep
8. Games and toys
9. Family
10. Just leadership

All of the tips outlined below are going to focus on these components so your dog can have the best life and training experience possible.

Choose the Best Food

When a dog is overweight, it affects their health and lifespan. The extra weight on your dog will put pressure on their joints, causing arthritis. Their risk for heart disease, tumors, and skin diseases increase. They will also stop exercising as much because they feel tired and out of breath sooner. This will only increase their chances of gaining weight because they won't run their weight off like they should.

Your veterinarian will talk about the best nutrition for your dog. They may also have food that you can purchase there. It's important to follow the diet that your dog's veterinarian prescribes as many dogs need a certain diet, especially if they are training.

Some of the best dog food brands include Natural Balance Original Ultra Whole Body Health, Horizon Complete, Whole Earth Farms, and Nature's Variety. These foods are generally more expensive than your traditional food, but they give your dog the best nutrients to keep their body healthy and bones strong.

Keep a Clean Living Environment

It's not only important that your environment is clean for the people in the home, but also for your furry family members. Animals will get into anything they can. They don't understand what is bad or good for them. Even if you see your dog sniff something bad for them and walk away doesn't mean they won't try it again. A clean living environment is a basic quality for a healthy life.
Another part to this is ensuring your dog is groomed. There are some breeds who need to be groomed on a weekly to monthly basis and others who can go a few months without seeing the groomer. If you don't want to take your dog to the groomer often, note how much they shed, if they need their fur trimmed, and other grooming factors before bringing your dog home. Give your dog a bath, trim their claws, and brush their coat.

Veterinarian Check-ups Are Important

Don't skip a check-up with your dog's vet! Even if they are healthy and happy, they need their annual check-up. Dogs that are in agility training and older should have a check-up at least twice a year. Once you bring your dog to their veterinarian, they will help keep you on track with any visits for your dog.

Keep Your Dog's Mouth Clean

Many people don't think of their dog's mouth when it comes to the animal's health. But, keeping their mouth clean is essential. Oral problems can cause pain for your pet and make it hard for them to eat or even drink water. Your dog's oral health can lead to kidney disease and increase their chance of death.
While most dog owners don't think it is necessary, it is important to brush your dog's teeth. You can give them a hard treat to help this process, but you should always take the time to brush your dog's teeth at least once a day.

Perform Weekly Health Checks Yourself

Once a week, check your dog's eyes and ears for any type of discharge or redness. Check your dog's skin and coat to ensure there are no signs of scabs, fleas, or ticks. You can always use medication to help prevent your dogs from getting fleas and heartworm. Your dog's veterinarian will help you get the right medication and shampoo for your dog. When your dog eats, watch for any signs that show they aren't eating or drinking like normal. If you notice anything different with your dog's eating or grooming habits, take them in for a check-up.

Tips to Overcome Training Challenges

There are a lot of challenges that happens during training. Most of them you will correct over time through training. For example, you need to call your dog's name a few times before they respond to you. This might happen because they aren't used to their name. It can also happen because they don't want to respond to you. Overcoming this challenge involves a training technique where you play the "name game."

Teaching Your Dog Their Name

There are various ways to teach your dog their name. One of the most common ways is known as the "name game."

1. Start calling your dog's name is a happy and fun tone when they are not looking at you.

2. When your dog turns to you, say their name again and give a verbal cue, such as "good" or "yes" followed by a treat.

3. Repeat this process for two to three minutes a few times a day.

4. Once your dog responds to their name after the first time you say it, stop saying your verbal cue and give them a treat.

5. Slowly decrease how often you give them a treat after saying their name. For instance, every other time, every third time, etc. until you stop giving them a treat.

You can use a different form of positive reinforcement for training. While a lot of people pick a treat, other people worry about their dog eating too many treats. Your dog can get sick if they take in too many treats a day. The best option for treats is to use small ones or break apart a larger treat.

Pulling on Their Leash

Another common trouble when training is your dog pulling on their leash. For example, you are talking to a friend while on a walk with your dog. Instead of your dog sitting there nicely until you decide to move again, your dog starts trying to pull you along with their leash. This is behavior that you need to stop for several reasons.

First, it doesn't show your dog the owner-dog relationship you should have. It places your dog in control and your dog cannot be in control when you train them as the training will not work. Second, your dog can hurt themselves by pulling. Third, your dog can get loose if the collar isn't on correctly.

To stop this behavior there are many forms of training you can use. For instance, you can teach your dog to sit, use a harness as that doesn't allow them to pull as much, or train them that when you stop, they stop. Most people like to teach their dog how to sit, but this doesn't mean that your dog will sit while you are talking. Teaching your dog to sit for a long period of time is a gradual training technique that will take months.

"Sit" is one of the first commands people teach their dog because it helps them in many situations. For instance, you can use it when you are taking a break on a walk or when your dog wants to jump on your company. There are several ways to teach your dog to sit, but these steps are the most common:

1. Get to your dog's level.

2. With a treat in your hand, hold it near their nose.

3. Tell your dog to "sit" and begin moving the treat up slowly. They will follow the treat with their eyes.

4. The more you move the treat, the closer their bottom will get to the floor. If they don't sit all the way down, gently push them down to sit. You need to watch how high you hold the treat because your dog will jump up if it goes too high.

5. Once your dog sits, even with your help, give them the treat and then praise them for sitting.

6. Like with other types of training, you will need to repeat this process regularly throughout the day.

Obedience School

No matter how much training you provide in your home, it is always a great idea to enroll your dog into obedience school. Not only will obedience classes help you train your dog, but you can receive support from like-minded people. You can also discuss any problems you are having with your dog's personal trainer.
When it comes to most obedience training schools, there are about four different levels. As your dog graduates from one level, you can enroll them into the next level. You do not have to enroll your dog in all four levels.

- Level one, basic skills: Level one focuses on the foundations of training, such as sitting, laying down, and get down. You will learn about training your dog to stay in their home base and walking your dog with a loose leash.

- Level two, building the skills: In this level, you will build on the skills your dog learned in level one. For instance, instead of sitting for a few seconds, your dog will learn to sit for a couple of minutes. They will also learn to automatically sit when you stop walking and coming to you when you call their name.

- Level three, advanced skills and special classes: Just like you do in level two, you will continue to build on your dog's previous learned skills. They will learn to sit and lay down for longer periods of time. You can also enroll your dog in special classes, such as agility training, hunting, therapy, and mental games.

- Level four, expert skills: In this level, your dog will learn to come when they are distracted. They will also learn how to wait at the door. This isn't just the door to your home; this is any door. For example, if you go to a neighbor's house and they invite you in, your dog will sit outside of their door until you come out. It is always important to keep your dog's safety in mind when leaving them out of your sight. While your dog reached the expert training level, situations can still arise. Most dogs in puppy mills are taken when dogs are left unattended outside.

Another trick your dog will learn at this level is to back up when they are in the way. It's common for your dog to walk in front of your feet and nearly trip you, especially at the puppy stage. Dog's don't understand that they can hurt you or you can accidently hurt them when they are in the way. This form of training alerts them to your movements and they will take a few steps back when they are in the way.

Find a Trusted Personal Trainer

Another tip to help you overcome challenges is to find a dog trainer that you can trust. Most dog trainers will take time to privately help you with training or allow you to email or call them when you are in need of assistance. You can ask them questions about how to overcome challenges or why your dog is reacting in a certain way.

Different Ways to Reward Your Dog

You always want to be cautious about how often you give your dog treats. They can get sick, especially if they have a sensitive stomach, from too many treats. Furthermore, if you focus on a lot of training throughout the day, your dog will fill up on treats and won't be hungry for their nutritious meal. Even if you have healthier treats, problems can still arise, such as your dog not wanting to eat their food because they want the treats instead. Therefore, it is best to come up with a different way to reward your dog other than using treats. Here are various forms of positive reinforcement:

Play a Game for a Few Minutes

Instead of a treat, you can play your dog's favorite game for a few seconds to a couple of minutes. If you are in the middle of training, you will want to keep playing brief. For example, your dog has a tug rope they love to play with. You bring this with you every time you and your dog are training. When they try to perform a step for a trick, even when they don't succeed, you take the toy and play with them for thirty seconds. Then, you go back to training. At the end of your training session, play with them for a longer period of time as this will start to alert your dog that their training session is now over.

Take a Trip to a Dog Park

If you decide to take a trip to a dog park at the end of each training session, you will want to have another type of positive reinforcement during the training. This might be playing a game for a few minutes or a treat. You don't want to wait to give your dog the positive reinforcement until they are done with their training session as this will make training harder. Dogs learn through positive reinforcement. Therefore, the more you use it, the stronger your dog will react to training.

Give Them Attention

Give your dog positive attention when they complete a training step. You can pet them and tell them how great they are, give them a hug, or any other type of attention. During the session, you want to keep the attention brief. Once the session is over, spend more time with them, just as you do when you play with them during training.

Preparing Your Dog for Training

There is a lot of information to remember when you are getting your dog ready for training. It's important that you do everything you can to start on the right side of training as this will help your dog learn quicker. It will also give you and your dog the best possible training experience.
Below are a few tips to follow before you start training. While some of these tips are specific to obedience classes, most of the tips associate with home training and obedience school.

Prepare Any Documents

When you enroll your dog into obedience school, you will need to have the correct documentation. For example, you will need papers from your dog's veterinarian that proves they are healthy enough for obedience classes. This includes proof that your dog had their shots.

Bring Your Dog for a Check-up

Let your dog's veterinarian know you are going to start training your dog. They will do a check-up to make sure that your dog is fit and healthy for their training. They will make sure that they received all their shots and give you tips on how to help your dog through the training process.
Most veterinarian clinics have booklets about training that they will hand you. This is free reading material to help you through the process. They can also inform you of your dog's diet and if it needs to change to ensure they remain healthy throughout the training process.

Understand Your Dog's Attention Span

Plan a little play and rest time between your training sessions. How long a training session can go will depend on the age of your dog. For instance, a puppy shouldn't sit through a whole session for longer than five minutes without a break. An older dog can go for about ten to fifteen minutes without a break. However, if you are outside on a warmer day, you will want to plan more water and rest breaks, so you dog doesn't become dehydrated or too warm.

The breaks don't need to be long. You can schedule about a minute or two for each break. This means that you will train your puppy for two minutes, then give them a minute break. Train your puppy for another two minutes, and then give them a minute break. Finally, you will train your puppy for another minute before ending the training session. You can repeat this type of session a few times a day. Some people set aside a time to train their dog in the morning and then in the evening. Other people focus on training their dog every two hours.

Make Sure Your Dog's Stomach is Empty

Don't feed your dog too close to a training session as this can cause them to have an accident. Even though accidents can still happen, you will decrease the chances. Try to have your dog use the bathroom before the training session starts, especially if you are bringing them to an obedience class. Your dog is more likely to feel alert and pay more attention when their stomach isn't full.

Have Everything Ready for the Training Session

If you are going to use treats or toys to during the training session, have them ready to go before you start training. It might be helpful, especially if you are just starting training, to hide the treats and toys so your dog doesn't notice them immediately. It can be harder to get them to follow your direction when they are distracted by their favorite objects and treats. You are also free to bring any treats and toys with you when you go to any obedience classes.

Keys for Successful Dog Training

Throughout this book, you will learn about a variety of tricks to teach your dog. Some of these tricks will be basic, such as potty training, shaking hands, and sitting while other tricks will focus on advanced training. No matter what type of training your dog is learning, you always want to keep these training keys in mind.

- Patience: All dogs learn at different rates. Don't feel that your dog needs to learn as fast as your friend's dog. If they learn slower, it doesn't mean something is wrong. It simply means that they take a little more time to learn and this is fine.

- Have realistic expectations: Don't go into training with the thought that your dog is going to learn everything right away. They are going to learn the tricks one step at a time, and it can take a couple of days or longer for them to catch on. Lower your expectations so you won't feel disappointed as your dog will catch on to this feeling.

Plan ahead: If your dog doesn't understand what you are trying to teach them, break the steps down even more. I try to keep the steps simple for your dog in this book, but there are still ways to help your dog learn in smaller steps. The goal is to set your dog up to succeed. If you need to plan out the steps differently, do this before you start training.

Always show kindness: Always be positive and use positive reinforcement when your dog is learning. Dogs want to impress their owners, they are going to try their best, but also make mistakes. The more kindness you show them, the more comfortable they will become and willing to listen to your commands.

Generosity goes a long way: While you always want to watch how many treats your dog consumes in one setting for health reasons, you can show as much positive reinforcement as you want. There is nothing wrong with giving your dog extra love, toys, and praises.

Always remain positive: If you start to feel frustrated, stop training and take a break. Your dog will only have enthusiasm for training if they see you are enjoying the process.

Practice, practice, practice: You want to practice the tricks your dog is learning and knows often. Remember to keep all training sessions short, but you can hold several throughout the day.

Set training goals: How are you going to know what you want your dog to achieve without training goals? Before you start training, take time to establish goals. Keep them realistic as this will help your dog thrive.

Stay away from discipline: Harsh punishment can cause your dog to feel afraid and interfere with training. If you want to correct your dog's behavior, focus on positive reinforcement techniques.

Reward your dog effectively: Your dog will become more motivated when positive rewards are enforced. Take time to give your dog positive attention, play with them, and show them that you are proud of their accomplishments and what they are achieving.

Chapter 3

Tips and Tricks for Training Your Puppy

The most common age for people to train their dogs is the puppy stage. This is also known to be the hardest stage because their attention span is short, and they are easily distracted. To have the best possible training experience, you will want to work with these factors and not try to force your dog to change what is natural for them at their age.

Know Your Puppy Before Training Begins

Before you bring your puppy home, start to do a little research. Get to know the main parts of your dog's personality by reading about their breed. All dog breeds tend to have their own characteristics, but your dog will also have their own personality. For example, your dog's breed might be on the shy side, but you notice your dog tends to warm up to people quickly. You then learn that not every dog from this breed is the same. In fact, most dogs remain hesitant around people they do not know.
Once you get your new family member home, spend time with them. You want to play with them, talk to them, and observe their behavior. Dogs need time to play and be by themselves and this is the perfect time to watch your dog's behavior. You also want to observe your dog's behavior when you are playing with them and when they are eating.

While you want to know the house rules before you bring your puppy home, if you want them to become comfortable quickly you will not become critical of them immediately. You won't harshly discipline them. Instead, you will understand that your puppy is learning their new environment and focus on giving them affection. You won't allow them to run wild in your home, but you will need to be patient when enforcing the rules.

When your dog is comfortable, they are going to listen to you better. They will follow your rules and the relationship between you and your dog will continue to grow strong. If you focus on rules before affection, your relationship will suffer. They will become more fearful of you, which can cause them anxiety. This will make training harder for both you and your dog. To correct your dog, keep your voice soft and start using simple words, such as "no." Always remember when your dog listens you should praise them with positive reinforcement.

Within a couple of weeks, you will have a good handle on your puppy's behavior. Expect their behavior to change as they grow, because it will. They will grow naturally as they age, with training, and becoming comfortable with their living environment. Once you feel your dog is comfortable and you should start to understand some of your dog's body language, which will help you understand your dog throughout the training process. For example, you will realize when your dog needs a break and when something is wrong.

The best time to start training a puppy is when they are a few months old. Professional trainers often say the best time to start training your puppy is between twelve to sixteen weeks old as this is known as the "golden period" (Klinger, 2019). This is the time when your dog will understand praise means they did something well, making them more likely to repeat the behavior.

One of the reasons it is important to get to know your puppy before training begins is that it allows them to get to know you. They will also understand certain pieces of their environment, making training a little easier over time. Once you feel your dog is comfortable in their new home with you and are old enough, you can start training your puppy with the basic foundations, such as home base, potty training, sitting, and going to bed.

Tips for Training Your Puppy

Puppies are quick to learn, but they can also cause a lot of stress in training. The key is to remember a few tips to make you and your dog's training experience the best.

Have Patience

Even though your dog is a quick learner, you will still need to practice patience. Puppies become distracted easily, they have trouble concentrating because of their short attention span, and they tend to be stubborn from time to time. This means that if your puppy doesn't want to focus on training, they are going to find something else to focus on.
You need to keep in mind that a lot of this is biological for your puppy. It takes time for them to learn how to read your behaviors and understand what you want from them. Don't become angry if your dog keeps becoming distracted during training. If this is frustrating, take a bit of a break and try again later. If you seem to have trouble gaining your dog's attention every time you are trying to start a training session, enroll them in an obedience school or talk to a professional trainer for advice.

Your Puppy Is at the In-Between Stage

Your puppy is not an adult or an infant. There are in-between stages when it comes to dogs. They are still developing mentally, physically, and emotionally and this can cause stress with training. At the same time, puppies can fool you. Because they are young, you may think they can't do a lot of tasks but think again. Puppies can do a lot more for themselves then they let on.
This age can also be tough for trainers because they struggle to know what their dog can handle and what it can't. The key to remember is that you need to take training one level at the time. Teach your dog the basics first, such as sitting, getting down, not jumping, laying down, and home base.

Train them on one trick at the time because they will become overwhelmed trying to learn more than one at once. Once they have a good hold on one trick, spend a couple weeks practicing this trick in your home and out in public. When they listen to you with very few mistakes, start training them on the next trick. Always remember to continue practicing the previous trick.

Your Puppy Has Fears

No matter how long you spend focusing on giving your puppy a comfortable home when they first come into your front door, they are going to be afraid. They may show you their fear and they may not. Some dogs try to hide their fear because they have a need to prove they are "fearless." Don't become concerned if your dog shows fear immediately. They are unsure of their new environment, you, and your other family members. They will need time to warm up.

During the puppy stage, they are going to act startled from time to time. This happens when they meet someone new or they hear a strange noise. You may see them jump, look around, sniff, and then continue on with their task. This is normal behavior for a puppy. When your dog doesn't seem to calm down and continues to show signs of fear is when you need to consider taking them out of the environment. Signs of fear include:

- Not eating or eating very little
- Not drinking water like they usually do
- Looking around the room
- Trembling
- Whining
- Trying to escape the area to avoid what is frightening them
- Diarrhea
- Unable to control their bowel movement
- Vomiting
- Panting excessively

- Salivating

If your puppy starts showing these signs and not letting up, it is time to take them out of the environment. Spend some time alone with your dog to comfort them and let them know that it is okay. Don't force them to go back into the environment if they don't have to. Chances are they will continue to feel afraid because something is causing them to feel this way.

If your dog is over five weeks old and continues to show these signs, they may have inherited fearful tendencies from one of their parents. In this case, you will need to talk to your dog's veterinarian or a professional trainer who can help you ease your dog's fears. This is important because your dog will remain fearful for the rest of their life if their fearful tendencies as a puppy are not taken care of.

Understand Your Puppy's Developmental Stages

In general, there are five developmental stages for puppies. Unless you have your dog from when they are born, you will not see all of the puppy's developmental stages. Once the puppy reaches their fifth stage, they are considered an adolescent dog.

Stage One: Neonatal Stage

Stage one occurs within the first two weeks after the puppy's birth. This is a crucial time for a puppy and their mother to bond. During this stage, it is essential that you check on the mother and her puppies to ensure they are healthy, and all puppies are eating, but don't focus on spending too much time with the puppies.

This is time for the mother and if the mother feels people are spending too much time with her puppies, she will become uneasy and want to move them somewhere else. The mother is the strongest influence for the puppy. They will begin to taste and touch right after they are born.

Stage Two: Transitional Stage

This stage starts when the puppy is two weeks old and goes until they are four weeks old. The puppy's behavior is heavily influenced by their mother. Therefore, you don't want to cause any stress on the mother. Even dogs feel overwhelmed by their new litter and are prone to aggression and depression easier. If your puppy feels this from their mother, they are more likely to show these characteristics later.

During this stage, the puppy will start to hear and smell. Their eyes will open, and they will start to stand, walk, bark, and wag their tail. At first, this won't happen a lot, but you will start to notice an increase in movement and sound coming from their location. Near the end of this stage, the puppy will see well, and they will start to show their teeth.

Stage Three: Socialization Stage

At this stage, puppies start to have longer stages of development. The socialization stage will start before the puppy is fully out of the second stage and it will last until they are twelve weeks old. During this stage, you want to make sure your puppy is getting all their social needs met, even if you don't bring them home until near the end of this stage.

There are several milestones during this stage:
1. Play time becomes important between three to five weeks old.

2. Puppies become more aware of their surroundings, people, and animals around them, and their relationships.

3. Puppies are highly influenced by their littermates between four and six weeks old. It is during this time they start to act more like a dog.

4. Starting at five weeks old, you need to make sure your puppy gets a lot of human interaction but start slowly. You don't want to overwhelm your puppy in the beginning because they

will be a bit frightened by every new person they meet. Try to ensure all the interactions with humans are positive as this time sets the tone for how the dog is going to react to humans throughout their life.

5. Curiosity increases and puppies start to get into everything. It's always a good idea to "puppy proof" your home. They will also need more supervision during this time period so they don't get into anything that can harm them.

6. The puppy's senses are fully developed starting at seven weeks. However, they will continue to work on their coordination ability. This is always a fun time to watch your puppy as they start to stumble and see what their small body is capable of.

However, watch to make sure they don't hurt themselves as they will try to go up and down the steps and jump onto any piece of furniture. If they see other pets or their mom doing something, they will want to try too!

7. Around week eight is when you want to start house training your puppy. The first step should be potty training.

Week eight is when your puppy will start to show true fear and the signs previously discussed. Spend a lot of time comforting your puppy when they become afraid.

8. Week nine is a great time to start training your puppy how to act around people. You always want to start small. They should understand the word "no" by this point. If they don't, it's a perfect time to incorporate this word into your training.

9. If they don't respond to their name, start the training process so they know to come to you when you call. It will help ease you and your puppy into more training in the next phase.

Stage Four: Ranking Stage

This stage starts at about month three and goes to six months. This is when the puppy starts to understand ranking, such as dominance and submission. Because of this, you want to start training your puppy and establish the owner-dog relationship. The more they understand that you are the one who gives them orders, the easier training will go throughout their life.

During this stage, you want to make sure your puppy has time to play with other dogs. Allow them to play with dogs of any breed and size. As long as they won't hurt your puppy, they will start to thrive in understanding the ranking system.

One of the biggest challenges during this stage is chewing. In general, puppies chew on everything because they are teething. Just like teething bothers babies, it bothers puppies. Unfortunately, there is very little people can do to help ease any teething pain. At the same time, you don't want them chewing on everything. Because they take part in the action so often, it's best to train them not to chew on unwanted items at this stage.

One way to keep a puppy from chewing on something they shouldn't is to distract them. This works because puppies are easily distracted. While some people state this doesn't directly teach them not to chew, it is important to realize this is a temporary stage for a puppy.

You also need to be very careful when training your dog not to chew because there are items they can chew on, such as a dog treat, bone, toy, etc. Some people will give their dog a chewing toy when they catch them chewing on a pillow. Over time your puppy will understand they are to chew on their toys and not the pillow. Remember to give them positive reinforcement every time they start chewing on their toy over another item.

You can also take the object they are not supposed to chew on away and say "no." You don't need to sound harsh when you say no, just directly stating the word lets your puppy know that they shouldn't chew on that item. The key is you need to be consistent. Another tip for chewing is to play more with your puppy. When dogs are tired, they tend to stay out of mischief.

Stage Five: Into Adolescence

The adolescent stage starts at about six months and lasts until eighteen months of age. There are more challenges with this stage than the previous stages because dogs tend to challenge people more during this time.

Foundation Training

Foundation training is the basic training techniques. During the puppy stage, you will want to focus on potty training and home base. You will focus on more foundation training during their adolescent months, which we will cover in the next chapter.

Potty Training

Potty training your dog will take a lot of time and it will be stressful. It's also a process that people tend to find what works for them. There are several ways to train your puppy to go potty. One of the key factors you need to remember is you want to pick a spot the first time you work on potty training and always use this spot. This could be a pad in your house or a spot in your yard.
Your dog will roam around and use the bathroom in other areas outside once they are a little older. When they are a puppy, you want to focus on one spot. Do not use newspapers. You want to have something that is sanitary for your puppy and your home.
1. Pick a spot: You want to choose a spot to lead your dog to when they need to use the bathroom before you start potty training. You can mark this spot, so you remember where it is, or other members of your family know where to bring the puppy. If you allow your puppy to roam in the yard during potty training, they are going to become too distracted and forget to go...that is, until they come back into the house.

2. Walk your dog to this spot every hour: Bringing your dog to the same spot will explain to them where they should go. Only stay in the spot for one to three minutes. If your dog uses the bathroom, reward them with positive reinforcement immediately. If they don't, take them outside in another ten to fifteen minutes. Repeat this process until they use the bathroom.

   Always remember what goes into your puppy will come out, and quickly. If they eat, take them outside when they are done. You will quickly learn that your puppy has a bit of a schedule when it comes to going potty. It will always help if you stick to a tight food and water schedule.
3. Longer breaks start at twelve weeks old: Around twelve weeks old, your puppy generally won't need to use the bathroom every hour. You can increase this time slowly, starting with one hour and fifteen minutes.

Remember, there will be accidents—a lot of them. However, when your dog starts having fewer accidents, it means they are catching onto potty training.

Bed Training

1. Have your puppy face their bed. Point your finger toward their bed and say "bed." You only want to give the command once as you want to teach your puppy to follow the command when you only say it once. Consistency not only means you give them the same verbal command every time, but also the same number of times. For example, if you say the first time, "bed, bed" you want to say that every time. Your dog can become confused if they hear "bed" one time and then "bed, bed, bed" the next time.

2. Once your dog gets into their bed, even if they don't lay down, give them positive reinforcement.

3. If they leave their bed, repeat the command just as you did the first time. Again, if they get into the bed, reward them.

4. Follow these steps for two to three minutes or until you puppy is becoming too distracted. Remember, they are learning and have a short attention span. This is where your patience comes in.

5. Once your dog goes to their bed and lays down when they are standing in front of the bed with you pointing and giving the command, back your dog away further away from their bed. You don't have to leave the room, but you want to be at least a couple of feet away from the bed. Repeat the process.

6. Once your dog is comfortable going to bed from a few feet away, practice this trick from the next room. You will continue to back further away from the bed the more your dog listens. The goal is they will go to bed when you say the command once, no matter where they are in their home base. Again, always reward them with positive reinforcement.

Home Base Training

Home base training is also known as perimeter training. This training teaching your dog where they can go and where they can't go. If you fear your dog running off because you don't have a fence or you don't want them going into certain rooms in your home, you will want to teach them this type of training. It is best they understand where they sleep (bed training) before you start their home base training as you can use their bed as the main home base point, meaning most of your training starts in this area.

Some people like to use the e-collar for this training because you can quickly alert your dog when they have gone too far without keeping them on a leash. However, you want to make sure your dog is old enough for the e-collar before this type of training. You can also use the clicker to alert them when they have gone too far. The key for the clicker is you want to be close to your dog, so you can give them a treat for coming back to their home base as soon as possible.

- Know where your dog can go and where they can't. Set up boundaries, such as cones or flags, to alert your dog when they have gone too far. It is important to stick to these boundaries. For example, can your dog go on the sidewalk? Can your dog go in the living room, bedrooms, and bathroom?

- Start by taking your dog around home base with the leash, clicker, or e-collar. When they pass the cones or flags, get their attention and give them the verbal cue of "no" or "home" and bring them back into home base. Repeat this step a few times until your dog stops going beyond home base as often.

- Bring their bed outdoors and place it in the middle of their home base area. Play with your dog, reminding them to come back to their bed when they pass home base. This step gives your dog a little more freedom and a specific location they need to go to when they pass the cones.

- Over time, you will notice your dog stopping near the cones. They might hesitate and then pass (remember, they are puppies and curious), but they should quickly come back when you call them.

- Use the bed as their specific location until they start running to it naturally when they cross the home base line.

- While your dog is in their home base area, walk beyond their perimeter line. This is basically a test to see if your dog follows you, if they hesitate, or if they wait for you to come back. The goal is to get your dog to wait for you, but this won't happen right away. A puppy is most likely to follow you because they don't like being alone. You can save this test until they are in the adolescent phase, but you want to keep it in mind for when the right time comes.

- Another test for your dog, when they are older, is to watch them as they are freely moving around your yard or home. Of course, you want to be close, so if they go beyond their perimeter, you can call them back.

One key factor to remember is no matter how well your dog is trained, stay in your yard. When they are outside you should supervise your dog. This is especially important when they are still puppies. They may run to chase a car or go up to people when they are walking by. Furthermore, your dog is going to become excited and anxious when they see another dog approach.
Another tip is to wait for home base training until your dog is an adolescent. This can be a difficult training technique for puppies to learn. It should be taught near the end of the puppy stage or the beginning of the adolescent stage.

Tucker's Perimeter Training

Max got Tucker when he was eight weeks old. The first week, Max focused on getting to know Tucker and allowing him to explore his new home. Max didn't worry about Tucker running off as he was always with his dog outside, but one day when Max talked to the mailman, Tucker dashed out the door and into the street.
Max quickly got Tucker's attention by calling his name, but he didn't understand what Max was saying. So, he sat on the road until Max picked Tucker up and brought him back inside.

After talking to the local dog trainer who operated the obedience school, Max enrolled Tucker in the first class and received about home base training. Fortunately, Tucker knew to go to bed when Max told him to, so Max decided to purchase cones and place them around his yard.

He then put Tucker on the leash and walked him around the yard. Whenever Tucker tried to go beyond the cones, he took out the clicker and pushed the button. Tucker looked at Max, who would say "home" and bring Tucker back inside the cones.

For the first week, Max simply walked Tucker around for two to three minutes. He always used the clicker, told Tucker "home," and gave Tucker positive reinforcement when he came back to home base. Soon, Max noticed Tucker didn't walk beyond the cones as often. They would repeat this about four times a day.

During the second week, Max decided to slowly decrease the use of the clicker. Max's goal for training was to say "Tucker, home" and his dog would return home. Using the same training schedule as the previous week, Max used the clicker every other time. By Wednesday, he used it once a day. When Friday came, Max got rid of the clicker.

During the third week, Max decided to get rid of the collar. He wanted to play outside with Tucker without having to keep him leashed. While Max felt a bit nervous, he remained calm every time Tucker took a step outside of the perimeter line. Once Tucker heard, "Tucker, home," he ran back to Max, who responded with positive reinforcement.

In the fourth week of home base training, Max decided to stop walking Tucker around and play with him while they were outside. Max became pleased to notice that Tucker rarely left the perimeter lines. If he got close, he would hesitate. Max watched to see what Tucker did before saying, "Tucker, home." Even when cars and other people went by, Tucker stopped and watched them, but he never left his home base.

In the fifth week, Max decided to test Tucker. One day, Max ran outside of the perimeter. He stopped and observed Tucker's behavior. With the cones still up, Tucker stopped and looked at the cones. He then looked at Max and sat down. Max ran back into the perimeter, gave Tucker positive reinforcement and tried the test again throughout the week.

Because Tucker only left the perimeter lines a couple of times during his test, Max decided to hide when Tucker was outside. He was close to Tucker's hearing range, so could quickly call Tucker back if he went beyond the cones. Tucker never left his home base.

The next week Max decided to take the cones down and observe Tucker's behavior. Tucker ran around the yard and sniffed where the cones used to be but remained in the perimeter. While Tucker did go beyond the established perimeter lines now and then, he always came back when he heard, "Tucker, home."

Chapter 4

Tips and Tricks for Training Your Adolescent Dog

Before you start training your adolescent dog, you want to make sure you get to know them, especially if they are new to your family. If you have had them for a while and started training your dog already, you will continue training into this stage.

Adolescence starts when your dog ends the puppy stage at about six months old. However, some people (including trainers) still call a dog a puppy until they are about eighteen months old as they don't recognize adolescence in dogs. For the purpose of this book, the time your dog is considered an adolescent is between six and eighteen months old.

What You Need to Know About Your Adolescent Dog

Just as children go through an adolescent stage, most people believe dogs do as well. During this stage, your dog is going through changes, including their hormones. This can make them act in ways that isn't their normal behavior. It's important to remember to stay calm during challenges. You also need to remember that your dog's brain is not fully developed yet. Below are other important factors to keep in mind through the adolescent years.

Teething Is Almost Over!

While your adolescent dog is still teething, the worst part is over. They are starting to move out of their teething phase, and you don't have to worry about them chewing on everything. However, you will want to ensure they still have a variety of chew toys to keep them occupied when they feel the need to chew. Dogs love to chew on their toys and keeping toys handy will ensure they don't think of touching your furniture when you are not there. But your dog is growing and with that, their chew toys need to grow. For example, if you gave them a bully stick a couple of months ago and it took them one hour to work their way through it, don't expect them to take an hour now. Purchase bigger chew toys or watch them closely when they are chewing on their smaller toys.

Bond, Then Bond Some More

Bonding with your dog doesn't end in the puppy phase. While they trust you and are comfortable in their environment, they need constant reassurance that they are important to you. Think of your relationship with your dog as constantly growing and getting stronger throughout their life. Of course, if you recently got your dog you should still be focusing on establishing a tight bond.
Make sure you are spending time playing with your dog. Talk to them as dogs love to have a conversation with their companions. Don't save up all your time for when you are training them. Always make sure you set aside specific play time with your dog.

Keep Your Dog Social

Even though your puppy has now hit the teen years, you still need to focus on socialization. This is especially important if you just brought your new family member home and are unsure of how much socialization they have received.

Enroll your dog in obedience classes as this will help them become social with other dogs and people. Take your dog to the park a couple times a week, if not more, for exercise and socialization. If you don't have another dog at home, try to find your dog some friends they can hang out with.

Keep in mind, your dog is still going to act fearful when something or someone is new to them. Continue to support and comfort your dog when they are afraid, and they will become used to the situation or understand the person is okay to be around.

Your Dog Is Not Going to Sleep As Much

Adolescent dogs don't need as much sleep as puppies. On top of this, their energy increases. Prepare yourself for busy days with your teen dog as they are going to keep you moving. Because of this, you want to keep them active throughout the day. Take them for a few more walks and play with them more. However, you don't want your dog to take part in any serious physical activity or sports yet. An adolescent dog's bones are still gaining their strength and they can easily break.

Did the Previous Training Fade Away?

If you taught your puppy to sit and you come to find that they don't sit as well as before, this is typical behavior for your adolescent dog. Mentally, dogs have a lot going on during this phase. They remember their previous training, but they can't seem to access everything they know right when they are supposed to. Continue to work on new training and practice the old training techniques you taught them so you can continue to build on them. Once your dog enters the adult phase, they will prove they remember everything you taught them.

Previous Dog Training?

If you just brought your dog home from the shelter, you won't know your dog's history. This means you won't know if they have had any type of training previously or not. Your best bet is to start with the basics or bring your dog to a dog behaviorist or trainer. They can give you information of what your dog may know, but without the cues your dog received from their previous trainer, it is hard to get your dog to follow your command.

Another option is you start training and find your dog catching on rather quickly over some types of training, such as laying down, but are slower to catch on to other types. This is a sign that they may have received training previously, but it wasn't consistent, or you aren't giving them the same cues.

Some people will tell you to start your dog's training from the beginning, just as you would a puppy. Even if they received previous training, you can retrain a dog in a different way, and they will follow your command.

Basic Training

If you just got your dog, you will want to start their training journey with sitting and home base training. If you received your furry friend as a puppy, you will want to continue training at this age. It's important to note that some of the training techniques I will discuss below can start at the puppy stage. Because there isn't a lot of time between the period you can start training the puppy at eight weeks and the period, they become an adolescent, the basic training mixes between the two phases. If your dog already knows to lay down, focus on the next type of training. If you are still working on teaching your dog how to sit, focus on this before moving on.

Come Training

Some people will teach them to come immediately after the dog learns their name. Other people will teach them after they learn to sit. The order you teach your dogs the basic commands depends on you. However, most trainers advise that learning their name and sitting should come first.

1. Start at your dog's home base by choosing a spot you want your dog to come to. Do your best not to move around until they show signs of understanding or you will confuse them.

2. Once you have your dog's attention, ask them to "come" and give them a hand gesture. Once they come to you, reward them.

3. Once they continuously come to you for a few training sessions, move around their bed, asking them to "come."

4. Next, place your dog in one room and go into the next room. While your dog can still see you, ask them to "come."

5. Once they do this repeatedly, move a little further away from their bed area and ask them to "come." At this point, you don't need to be in their line of vision but want to make sure you have their attention.

6. Follow up "come" with an additional command your dog already knows, such as "sit." For example, you will ask your dog to come. Once they come to you, give them a little positive reinforcement. Next, you will ask them to "sit." Once they sit, follow up with more positive reinforcement.

Lay Down Training

1. Make sure your dog knows their home base before you start training. You will want to follow this step with every basic

training method we discuss in this chapter. It is also helpful for some intermediate and advanced techniques, but not all.

2. Call your dog into their home base, usually where their bed is, by gaining their attention. If they understand "come" use that or call them by their name. When they come into their home base area, give them positive reinforcement.

3. You don't want to make your dog think you are telling them to go to bed. You want to keep "bed" and "lay down" separate because they are not always going to be in bed when you tell them to lay down. You might be at a friend's house, outside, in obedience school, or at the park. You want to get your dog used to laying down in any situation.

4. Ensure you have your dog's attention and say "lay down" with a hand gesture. You want this to be different than the gesture to "sit" or "come." It might help to get your dog to "sit" first and then get them to lay down. Like you did with sitting, you might need to gently push your dog down or lower a treat to get them to lay down fully. Remember to reward them, even for the smallest effort.

5. Once your dog is constantly laying down when you give the command, start practicing in other areas around your home and outside. You can even take them to stores that allow dogs and work on saying "lay down" when there are distractions around them.

6. Do your best to make sure your dog remains in the lay down position for a few seconds, As you continue to practice throughout the months you will increase the time, they remain in the lay down position slowly. This will also be a part of most obedience classes.

At first, it is important that you don't force your dog to lie down for a long period of time. This can cause them to feel stressed as they are highly active dogs at this point. Even if they stay in the lay down position for a couple of seconds, make sure you give them positive reinforcement.

Case Example: Brick Learns to Lay Down

Tamara brought her dog, Brick, home when he was eleven weeks old. Over the last few months, she has taught him home base, come, and sit. She is now working on teaching Brick to lay down. As a positive reinforcement, Tamara uses treats. She also uses the clicker in order to get her dog to follow her command along with a verbal command.

Tamara starts the three-minute training process by calling Brick into his sleeping area. Once he comes, she gives him a treat. With the clicker in her hand, Tamara says, "Brick, sit." Brick responds by sitting, so she rewards him with another small treat. She then says, "Brick, lay down," and places her hand on his shoulder and brings a treat near the floor. As Brick is following the treat, she gently guides him down on the floor. Once he is laying down the whole way, she gives him a treat.

When Tamara stands up, her dog stands up and she tries the process again. This time, instead of placing her hand on the dog's shoulder, she uses the clicker and places the treat close to the floor. When Brick lays down the whole way, she gives him the treat. At this point, the three minutes are up. Tamara gives Brick some much needed attention as more positive reinforcement.

A couple of hours later, Tamara calls Brick into his sleeping area again. She repeats the training method with the clicker for another three minutes. Tamara and Brick go through this process four times a day. Within a week, Tamara is training Brick to lay down in other places around his home base. The following week, Tamara brings Brick to the park where they practice laying down when Brick gets excited about meeting a new person.

Stay Training

Just like with lying down and sitting, your dog won't stay for a long period of time. They may only come and stay for a couple of seconds. Even so, you want to reward their efforts with positive reinforcement. You can work on slowly increasing their stay time over the next few months.

1. To start training, call your dog into their home brace area. This is a great opportunity to practice "come" training. Once your dog follows your command, reward them with positive reinforcement.

2. Tell your dog to "sit" but do not give them their positive reinforcement right away. Instead, place your hand on the top of your dog's head and say "stay."

3. Give your dog positive reinforcement by playing with them to get them back up again.

4. Repeat the sit command and then say "stay" and wait a couple of seconds to ensure that they stay. Reward your dog.

5. Continue this process and gradually increase the amount of time your dog stays.

6. Once your dog is sitting for about five to ten seconds, take a couple of steps back. Even if your dog moves, reward them for the effort.

7. Continue to take a couple of steps back from your dog once they stay for a short period of time. For example, if your dog stays for ten seconds after you take a couple of steps back, the next time that you focus on stay training, take a couple of more steps back. Eventually, you will leave the room and see if your dog stays. Don't keep your dog staying alone in the room for too long because they might start to worry. This is

another trick that you will gradually increase the amount of time your dog stays.

8. Once your dog is comfortable with the "stay" task, you will want to add in other commands, such as lay down.

Case Example: Allie Learns to Stay

Amirah brought her dog, Allie, home a few months ago and started training her a couple weeks later. Now, Allie is in level two of a local obedience class, so Amirah is working on getting Allie to stay as this is what they are working on in class.

Amirah calls Allie into her sleeping area and gives her positive reinforcement by giving Allie a few seconds of attention. Amirah then stands back up and tells Allie to "sit." Once Allie listens to the command, Amirah tells Allie "stay" and holds up her hand in front of Allie's face as a hand gesture. After a couple of seconds, Amirah rewards Allie.

Once again, Amirah tells Allie to "sit" and "stay" as she raises her hand. At this point, Amirah decides to take a couple steps back. While Allie seemed like she was going to get up, she sat back down and stayed there until Amirah rewarded Allie with positive reinforcement.

After a few hours, Amirah called Allie back into her sleeping area and practice "sit" and "stay" again. This time, Amirah took several steps back, but Allie stood up and followed. Amirah rewarded Allie for her efforts with positive reinforcement and tried again, this time sticking to a couple of steps back. After a couple of times, Amirah moved four steps back, Allie didn't move until Amirah gave her positive reinforcement.

After a week, Amirah decided to add the command "come" after telling Allie to "stay." However, Amirah only said, "Allie, come," after taking about five to seven steps back. The next week, Amirah went into the next room as Allie stayed near her sleeping area. Allie didn't move until she heard her companion say, "Allie, come."

Get Down Training

It is easier to train your dog to get down when they jump up on something. Therefore, you don't need to start this training in a specific location as you want to catch them in the act.

1. Once your dog jumps up on something or someone, say "down" or "off" while you are showing them a treat in your hand.

2. When your dog gets down, reward them with the treat.

3. It is important that everyone gives your dog positive reinforcement. For example, your dog jumps on your friend who walks in the door. You respond by telling your dog "off" and show him the bag of treats you have handy. Your dog gets down and you give him a treat. At the same time, your friend gives him some attention.

You will find it hard to always have treats handy whenever your dog jumps up on something they shouldn't. You can always use a different type of training, such as the e-collar, to train your dog to get down. However, you will still need to show some type of positive reinforcement, such as playing with your dog when they get down.

Case Example: Matt's Get Down Training

Donnie brought Matt home about four months ago. Since Matt knows how to sit, lay down, and come, Donnie has started to focus on telling Matt to "get down" when he jumps on people as they walk in the front door. Because Matt only jumps on people as they enter the door, Donnie decided to keep treats by the door.
Every time Matt jumps on someone, including Donnie, he grabs the treats bag right by the door and says "down." The problem Donnie runs into is that it doesn't work for him because Matt becomes interested in the treats and won't get down through verbal command.

Because Donnie can't keep Matt's "get down" training consistent, he needs to figure out a different way. After some research, Donnie decides that Matt is old enough of an e-collar.

Once the e-collar comes, Donnie places the e-collar on Matt and allows him to get used to it for the first week. When the day came for training, Donnie told Matt "down" when he jumped on him. When Matt didn't respond, Donnie pressed the button on the e-collar to send Matt the signal. Immediately, Matt got down and shook his head a little. Donnie rewarded Matt for getting down.

Within the first week, Donnie noticed that Matt started hesitating before he jumped up on someone. Donnie only sent the signals to Matt if he didn't get down after Donnie said "down."

Real Life Training

It's important to train your dog in a controlled and uncontrolled setting. A controlled setting is your home as you can control the area you train your dog, who is around you, and most distractions. The trouble with this is, if you are going to take your dog into certain stores, out to the park, or for walks, you can't just train them a controlled setting. You also want to train them in a real-life setting.

There are a lot of surprises that can pop up when you are in public with your dog. One of the greatest ways to prepare for these surprises is to practice training in public. To give you more of an example, let's look at how Roger trains his dog, Gidget at the local pet store:

After bringing Gidget home from the animal shelter two months ago, Roger is focusing on teaching his dog to stay. After training Gidget is at home for a couple of weeks, Roger decides to take her to the pet store so they can pick up more food, treats, and a new chew toy for Gidget.

While she is on her leash, Roger is looking at the dog treats when Gidget starts to move around. Roger looks down at her and says, "Gidget, sit." She looks up at Roger and sits down. Roger praises his dog, but notices that she is distracted by something else.

Looking in that same direction, Roger sees a larger dog a few feet away. It is at that moment Roger starts noticing that Gidget is acting a little strange. As he observes her, she seems to be getting anxious. The larger dog doesn't seem like a threat, but Roger knows that anything could have happened in Gidget's past.

Roger tells Gidget that it is okay, but she keeps her eyes on the larger dog, who takes a couple more steps toward Gidget. At that moment, she stands up and starts to head towards the larger dog with a slight growl. Gently, Roger says, "Gidget, sit." When Gidget doesn't respond, Roger stands in front of Gidget, to try to block her view of the larger dog.

Again, Roger says, "Gidget, sit." Gidget sits, but then stands up before Roger can praise her. Roger repeats calmly, "Gidget, sit." Once she sits down, Roger quickly says, "stay," and holds up his hand. Gidget stays sitting and Roger praises his dog. By the time he is done giving her attention, the larger dog is gone.

As the story about Roger and Gidget shows, you never know what is going to happen in a real-life setting. This is one of the biggest reasons you want to do enough training at home that you can use different techniques. One of the techniques Roger used is called blocking and it is a popular trick to use when you don't want your dog seeing something or someone that can cause them to become anxious or aggressive.

What to Do With Aggressive Dogs?

Whether it is your dog that becomes aggressive or another dog, you want to try to stop the situation as quickly as possible. The best way to do this is by knowing the signs of an aggressive dog. Some of the signs include:

- A stiff body
- Growling
- Snarling
- Biting
- Ears are pinned back

If you notice someone else's dog acting this way while you are walking your dog, try to get your dog to go a different direction. You might need to distract your dog or block them from seeing the dog to get them to go in a different direction.

Beyond Basic Training

Near the end of your dog's adolescent stage, you may start teaching them tricks that aren't considered basic. Some of these are advanced tricks to help your dog act their best while other tricks are for fun. These tricks can be games, dog sports, hunting, or anything else that is interesting to you and you believe your dog will enjoy. There are over a hundred dog tricks available at your fingertips.

Unless you are training your dog for agility training or hunting, any training beyond the basic training should be strictly fun for your dog. If you start training them on a certain trick and they don't seem interested, move on to a different trick. With so many tricks, it is possible that your dog is not going to enjoy all of them. If your dog needs to learn them, then work on it like you did with basic training. If they don't need to learn them, it is important you don't force them as this can lead to a difficult training period.

Pulling on the Leash

Dogs tend to pull on the leash when they are on walks or not interested in staying in the area they are supposed to in the backyard. When dogs pull on their leash, they can hurt themselves or get loose and go missing.

The main reason they pull on the leash is because they have a place they want to go, but they are unable to get there because you don't have the same idea, or they can't go beyond a certain point. It doesn't matter what size your dog is, pulling on the leash can be dangerous. Therefore, it is always in your dog's best interest to train them not to do this.

One of the best tips for training a dog not to pull is to keep them interested in their surroundings. Take your dog for a brisk walk and change your direction frequently. This causes your dog to pay more attention to their surroundings as you are offering more for your dog to look at. When this happens, they aren't going to get bored or start focusing on a specific location and become determined to get there.

1. Once you get your dog walking briskly behind you, look to notice when they turn to follow you. When this happens, stop and give your dog positive reinforcement. A lot of people will use the clicker during this training because your dog will associate the click sound to them turning to follow you. They will then associate the positive reinforcement to the click, bringing their training into a full circle. If you don't use a clicker, use a verbal command, such as "good," "yes," or "turn." Remember to use a verbal cue that you don't use for any other type of training.

2. After your dog comes to follow you without pulling on the leash, get a longer leash to see if your dog will become distracted and go the other direction. If your dog does, stop, get their attention, and then give them positive reinforcement for coming to you. This is a great time to incorporate the "come" command. If your dog follows, continue walking but give them positive reinforcement at the same time.

3. As time goes on, start choosing busier places to walk and walk a little faster. Repeat the training steps to ensure your dog understands that no matter what is going on in their environment or what they want to see, they need to follow you when you are walking.

A Digging Dog

Dog's dig for many reasons. First, some breeds feel the need to dig because it is instinctive. They were bred to dig for food and other animals. Second, dogs dig because they are bored, lack of exercise, wanting to cool off more during a hot day, or frustrated.

Before you start training your dog to stop digging, you need to understand why they are digging. German Shepherds, Beagles, Huskies, and Terriers are dogs where digging is part of their instincts. When it comes to this, it's hard to teach them not to dig. You might even find yourself questioning if you should try to stop them from digging because it is part of their nature. However, you also need to consider your yard, the yards of your neighbors, and other factors.

Typically, if your dog is bred to dig, they will still do so now and then as training is going to be harder for them. However, if your dog does this because they are bored or need a stress reliever, training will be easier, especially if you work with your dog and keep them busy if they are bored and calm if they are stressed.

If you have a dog whose instinct is to dig, you can think about getting a sandbox or some other type of digging area for your dog. During your training, you can focus on taking your dog into this area to dig instead of digging in various places within your yard. Of course, your dog will still need supervision to ensure that no inappropriate digging happens.

1. Cover a digging area for your dog with sand or loose soil. To make the area more appealing to your dog during a hot day, give the area protection from umbrellas or place the area in a shaded space.

2. Bury your dog's toys and allow them to start going on a treasure hunt.

3. Every time they dig in the digging area, give your dog positive reinforcement. Do not punish your dog for trying to dig in an inappropriate area.

4. If you struggle with getting your dog to stop digging in the wrong area, make it unattractive by adding rocks.

5. Supervise your dog whenever they are outside so you can lead them into the correct digging area and praise them.

If your dog is bored or needs more exercise, you can follow the training steps and increase your dog's activity level. For example, take them on longer walks, play with them more, give them interesting outside toys that they can play with. It is helpful to keep the outside toys separated from the inside toys, so they don't become bored with the toy quickly.

Tug and Release

Tug and release is a game that you should teach your dog before you focus on fetch. Use can use tug and release as a way to help your dog learn one of the steps in fetch.

For this game, it is best to have two identical soft toys or ropes that your dog can tug on when you are gently trying to pull it out of your dog's mouth. You never want to pull hard on a toy when it is in your dog's mouth because you can hurt them. It is possible for your dog to pull hard enough that their teeth become loose.

The best verbal cues to use are "grab it," "tug," and "drop it." You will also use the visual cue of waggling the toy to get your dog interested in the game.

1. Hold the toy in front of your dog but wait for them to look at the toy. Once they do, give them positive reinforcement.

2. Once your dog grabs the toy with its mouth, say "grab."

3. Let your dog pull the toy out of your hand while you are holding it. Make sure that you are holding it lightly, so your dog won't hurt themselves. Give your dog positive reinforcement.

4. Grab the toy and gently pull. Whenever you pull, exclaim with enthusiasm, "tug!"

5. If your dog doesn't drop the toy, bring out the identical toy and get him interested in his. Once your dog drops the toy in his mouth, say "drop."

6. Allow your dog to grab the second toy and repeat the process. Each time you get to the "drop" step, start to say it a little earlier as this will teach your dog to drop the toy when you say "drop."

There are dogs that will do everything they can to keep the toy in their mouth. They won't let go when you show them the identical toy. If this is the case, have treats on hand. When you say "drop" toss a treat on the floor and then praise them.

Teaching Your Dog to Play Fetch

Most people find teaching their dog to play fetch relatively easy. It is almost like an instinct to some dogs. It's easy to teach your dog to play fetch by focusing on positive reinforcement instead of the clicker, treats, or the e-collar. However, if you have a dog that likes to run off from home base, you might want the added security of the clicker or e-collar, especially if this is the way you are teaching your dog to stay at home base.

There are three main verbal cues you will use when teaching your dog to fetch:
1. "Get"
2. "Bring"
3. "Drop"

Some people like to use "give" instead of "drop." The problem with this is your dog can end up biting someone or scratching a little hand with their teeth. They won't mean to do this; they will be excited and have trouble containing themselves. Furthermore, if your dog likes to play a game of tug-o-war, they might think of this game when you are trying to get the ball, frisbee, or other item out of their mouth.

1. Find two toys that look exactly the same or purchase two of the same toys.

2. Keep one toy behind you where your dog can't see it and the other toy in front of your dog.

3. Tease your dog with the toy. You don't need to tease your dog for a long period of time, just for a few seconds or a minute. The point is to get them excited to run for the toy when you toss it.

4. Once your dog shows interest in the toy, toss the toy a few feet and say "get." You don't want to toss it very far at first because you want to get to your dog as soon as possible so you can praise them when they have the toy in their mouth.

5. This step is one of the hardest parts of teaching your dog fetch because they are not used to bringing the toy back. To do this, say their name and add "bring" to the end. For example, "Buddy, bring." When your dog takes a couple steps in your direction, praise them by grabbing the toy in their mouth and playing tug with them for a few seconds. You want to make sure you drop the toy before they drop it. You want the toy to remain in their mouth.

6. Once you get back to training, show your dog the identical toy from behind you. Start teasing them with the identical toy. Once they drop the toy in their mouth, say "drop" and praise them before throwing the identical toy.

7. While they are running to get the identical toy, pick up the toy that was in their mouth.

8. Repeat the process.

9. Once your dog starts to understand the process of fetch, you will start to combine the words "get," "bring," and "drop" into fetch. This is when you throw the toy and you say "Buddy, fetch." When your dog has the toy in their mouth, tell them to "bring" it. When they come, tell them to "drop" it. At this point, you will praise them once they drop the toy before continuing to play the game.

Peekaboo

Not all dog tricks need to take a serious tone. Other than fetch, there are a lot of other fun games you can teach your dog, such as peekaboo. This is a trick where you have to think of safety and size of your dog because they will stand between your legs. Only teach your dog this trick if they are small enough to fit between your legs when you are standing. You also want to make sure your legs are far apart, but you are comfortable enough, so you don't lose your balance and end up stepping on your dog.

While this trick seems easy enough, and most dogs get it within a few days, going between legs can be frightening to some dogs.

1. With your legs wide apart, command your dog to "sit" and "stay" behind you.

2. With a treat between your fingertips, reach it through your legs and toward your dog.

3. Try to not let your dog receive the treat or positive reinforcement until they are halfway through your legs.

4. Once you see your dog and right before you give them the treat, say "peekaboo."

5. If they are scared, drop the treat between your legs and give them positive reinforcement for trying.

6. When you repeat the trick, you want to focus on saying "peekaboo" earlier each time. The idea is that the cue for your dog to come between your legs is "peekaboo" and not the treat.

7. As your dog becomes more comfortable, you can move your legs closer together. Always ensure your dog can get through your legs without knocking you down or you stepping on your dog.

8. When your dog starts responding to the "peekaboo" cue, slowly decrease the times you use a treat to lure them between your legs.

Boing

When your dog is an adolescent, you are going to think about the various types of training for your dog. If you are interested in agility training, such as dog sports, you can start by teaching your dog to jump over a bar. Boing is also a great trick to teach your dog if you notice they have trouble with jumping or don't jump high enough. The best verbal cues to use with this trick are "boing" or "jump."

1. You want to lure your dog to jump. Most people do this by holding a treat between their fingertips, so their dog can see.

2. Get down to your dog's level by crouching and then spring up onto your tiptoes. When you jump up, raise your arm as this will get your dog to jump for their treat.

3. When you see your dog jump with you, say "boing."

4. Allow your dog to get the treat and give them positive reinforcement.

5. The next time your crouch down and jump up, raise your arm up a little higher. You want to gradually increase the length your dog jumps. If they are frightened of jumping, start lower, such as going from the floor to a little above their head.

6. You want your dog to learn to jump as high as possible, but not to the point they may hurt themselves coming down. If your dog is older, they may not jump as high. Senior dogs shouldn't jump as it can cause more damage to their joints, especially if they have arthritis.

Time Out

While this trick is called time out, it isn't meant to be a punishment for your dog, though some people use this trick as such. One reason people teach their dog time out is because it can allow your dog to know that they need to calm down. Dogs are easily excited when there are other people around. Larger dogs can easily become overwhelming for young kids. If there is every moment where you want your dog to calm and show off their skills at the same time, this is a trick to teach your dog.

Time out is when your dog will lay on their side with their legs stretched out. To give them the visual cue, you hold your hand out flat, lay your hand in front of your dog, and flip your hand from palm up to palm down. The verbal cue is either "down lie" or "time out." Most professional dog trainers will refer to this trick as "down lie."

1. At first, this trick may be easier to teach your dog in steps they already know. For example, first tell them to "sit." After giving them some positive reinforcement, tell your dog to "lie down."

2. Once your dog is on the ground on all four legs, go to one side of your dog with a treat. You want to help your dog lay flat on their side. You can do this by holding a treat close to

your dog's face and the luring it toward their shoulder. Their head will follow the treat.

3. You can start this trick with smaller steps. For example, once your dog sits on their hip, you give then a treat. Your next step will be to get them halfway laying on their side. Then, fully laying on their side with their legs stretched out.

4. Once your dog is laying flat on their side, say "time out" and give them a treat.

5. When your dog starts to react to the treat, add in the visual cue. Your goal is to get rid of using the treat and use the visual cue instead.

Roll Over

Like time out, roll over is another trick that you can teach your dog in smaller steps. You can also start with using the tricks your dog already knows, such as sit, lie down, or time out. The visual cue you will use is pointing toward your dog and making a circle with your finger. The verbal cue you use is "roll over."

1. Command your dog to sit.

2. Kneel in front of your dog with a treat between your fingertips.

3. Command your dog to lay down.

4. Command your dog to time out.

5. Lure your dog to roll over half-way by placing the treat by their nose, moving it towards their shoulder, and then slowly to the other direction. For example, if your dog is lying down facing east, you want to move your treat west. Your dog will follow the treat, making them go into a belly-up position and then reward them.

6. Start your dog back at the beginning and then practice having them roll over slowly, going a little farther to complete the roll over trick each time. Give your dog the treat and then positive reinforcement each time.

7. Once your dog fully rolls over with treats, introduce the visual cue. Keep using the treats at first. When your dog starts to roll over by following the visual cue, slowly decrease the treats you use to get your dog to roll over.

Hunting

Near the end of the adolescent stage, or at the beginning of the adult stage, most people start to train their dog for hunting. There are several breeds of dogs that are great hunters. In fact, it is often a part of their instincts and they are happy when they are hunting.

If you decide to get a dog and teach them to hunt, you want to look into getting an e-collar. There are specific hunting e-collars that will reach your dog to a mile in length. They can be a great tool as you can train your dog to go back home or come back to you when you send them the signal.

1. The first step you want to do is map out your hunting route. You want to make sure that you have a clear route from your home or vehicle to where you will hunt. You will also want to plan out the route you will take in the woods while you are hunting. If you don't know the woods well, mark your route in various places, so you can be sure to learn it as well.

2. Teach your dog the hunting route. Take them along the path a few times and let them see where your hunting base is. Allow them to get used to the smells of the route. Take your time so they become comfortable along the route.

3. Train your dog to return home. This will ensure that no matter what happens, especially if they go beyond the e-collar range, that they won't get lost. However, it is always

best to have your dog in your sight or give them a signal as soon as you lose sight of your dog. Dogs can run fast, and it won't take them very long to get beyond a mile.

4. Retrain your dog on hunting every year before you take your hunting trip. Repetition is key, and while your dog will remember everything about hunting, it will help when it comes to the route. Things can change along the route in a year and if a tree falls or something else happens, your dog can become confused along the route. Furthermore, the smells are not going to be the same from year to year.

Chapter 5

Tips and Tricks for Training Your Adult Dog

Around eighteen months is when your dog enters adulthood. They will remain in this stage until they become a senior dog, which is anywhere between six to ten years old. By this age, you should be done introducing basic training, but still working on building the skills.

For example, you will teach your dog to stay longer over a period of time. Of course, if you just brought home your dog from the shelter, you will need to start with the basic training discussed previously.

While you will focus on the training tips discussed previously, your adult dog can train for a longer period of time. Instead of two to three minutes, you can go about four to six minutes. At the same time, you may need more patience. An adult dog has spent over a year or more going about their life a certain way, whether they were trained or not.

For instance, you got your dog from the animal shelter. One of the first traits you notice about your dog is they pee on paper they find lying around the house. You assume that this is because the previous owners allowed their dog to pee on newspaper. Therefore, you need to house train your dog to use the bathroom outside instead of paper they find around the house. This training can take longer than it would for a puppy because they have gone to the bathroom by using paper for a period of time.

Keeping Your Adult Dog Healthy

Focusing on keeping your adult dog healthy is a little different than a puppy or adolescent dog. First, you need to watch their weight more. Another factor is you have to make sure that you follow your dog's veterinarian's orders if they tell you to start your dog on any type of medication or vitamins. The more you focus on keeping your dog healthy and fit, the longer your dog will live. Here are a few tips for keeping your adult dog healthy:

Make Sure You Are Feeding Your Dog the Right Food

Diets for adult dogs are different from younger dogs. You may need to look into special diet food to keep your dog's weight under control. Because adult dogs aren't as active as puppies or adolescents, they tend to gain weight a little faster. This causes a lot of health problems over a period of time and will shorten their lifespan.
If you aren't sure what food is best for your dog, talk to your dog's veterinarian. This is especially important if your dog starts to develop signs of a disease or illness. While this specialty food is a little more expensive than common name brands, keeping your dog healthy and extending their lifespan is worth it.

Include Healthy Activities Into Your Dog's Schedule

Making sure your dog stays active is something you want to do throughout their life. However, as your dog ages, you will need to spend more time making sure your dog remains active. During this age, you can start to teach them how to play fetch, if you don't during their adolescent years. You can also teach them various games to play to keep their mind and body active.

Track Your Dog's Weight

Most veterinarians will start to tell you to track your dog's weight once they reach adulthood. This is because your dog can lose or gain weight rapidly. There are a lot of reasons for this and if you find your dog losing or gaining weight at a fast pace, you need to bring them in for a checkup. However, if they start losing weight at a slow pace, you shouldn't have to worry unless they begin to lose too much weight.

Increase Your Visits to the Veterinarian's Office

When dogs are young, most veterinarians only want to see them annually. Once your dog reaches adulthood, they will start to request more frequent visits. This might start at twice a year and then go to three times a year when they get closer to reaching the senior age. Make sure you follow the veterinarian's advice with how often they want to see your dog. If any type of health problem arises, you can catch it quickly and take care of it to increase your dog's lifespan.

Adult Dog Training Techniques

Before you start training your older dog, your dog needs to be comfortable in their environment. They need to know that you are there to help them and give them what they need to have a healthy and happy life.
If you recently received your dog from an animal shelter, you don't know anything about your dog's past. However, it is possible that your dog comes from a negative past where they were abused and neglected. This is going to affect your dog mentally, emotionally, and physically. It's important that you take everything slowly when bringing an adult dog home because they can have years of heartache and pain built up inside of them.

You never want to react harshly in any way, no matter what your dog does. You need to give them time to adjust before you start training. Even if they aren't well potty trained, be patient and kind with their accidents. The more you show your adult dog love and compassion, the stronger the bond will form. This won't help them get over any trauma from their past, but it will help them know that they are in a much better home.

Your dog's past can be the biggest challenge when it comes to training. If they dealt with abuse, they will have a hard time following commands. They might be more interested in watching your every move to make sure they can protect themselves because they are still learning how you are going to react and treat them.

If you start to feel frustrated, your dog is going to pick up on this and become increasingly anxious. You should only train a dog, especially older dogs who could have lived through trauma, when you are happy and calm. The moment you start to feel this slip away is the moment you need to cease training. Ensure you always end it by giving your dog positive reinforcement.

If you feel your dog is really struggling and shows signs of anxiety, depression, or fear, consider taking them to a dog behaviorist. They will help you and your dog overcome any of their trauma so your dog can start to heal and lead a healthy and happy life.

Training Tips for Older Dogs

Age Doesn't Matter

No matter how old your dog is, they can learn just as much as a puppy. Many people believe that an older dog cannot learn new tricks; this is a myth. Dogs love to learn and please their owner at any age. While you will need more patience and teach your dog at a slower pace than a puppy, your adult dog will quickly thrive in their new learning environment. You will be proud to show off all of the new tricks your dog knows.

Use a Crate

It's not always a favorite for people because they feel a crate cages their dog like a jail, but, to your dog, it can be a comfortable place to sleep and relax. This is especially true for older dogs who like to make sure they have a sense of security around them.

Build Your Dog's Confidence

If you recently brought your older dog home from a shelter, you want to focus on building their confidence before you start training them regularly. Dogs are going to focus more on their training and believe they are pleasing their owners if they have a higher self-confidence. Most people don't think about a dog's mental state, but how they feel about themselves and their surroundings is one of the strongest indicators for their success. Your dog is always going to try to please you, but by feeling more confident in themselves and their abilities, they will believe you are proud of them.

Back Up

Back up is when you teach your dog to walk backwards. This is a great trick if you find your dog in the way or you want to practice teaching them a new trick to keep their mind and body active. Most dogs understand this trick fairly quickly. The verbal cue you will use is "back" and the visual cue is waving your hand in the "leave" or "go away" motion.
If you want your dog to back up in a straight line, you want to set up a space where your dog will back up. This could be placing cones down the center of a hallway and allow your dog to walk between the cones and one side of the hallway.
You can even add to this trick. If you want your dog to learn agility training have your dog back up while weaving between the cones. However, this will come later as you want your dog to start by backing up in a straight line and then backing up between the cones. Remember, you always want to take little steps in training.

1. Stand at the entrance of the hallway. Have you back toward the hallway and your dog in front of you.

2. With a treat, lure your dog to follow you a few steps into the hallway. You will want the treat close to their nose.

3. After a few steps, stop, and take a few steps forward to make your dog back up. You can help your dog do this by putting the treat above their head and slowly moving it behind their head. If your dog turns around, give them a treat for effort. If your dog follows the treat by taking a couple steps back, give them the treat by tossing it between their front paws. This will make them back up a bit more.

4. Once your dog backs up with the treat, add the verbal cue of "back" when they start walking backwards.

5. Slowly decrease the treats and focus on using the verbal cue. However, have a treat in your hand for positive reinforcement.

6. Add in the visual cue of waving your hand when you say "back."

7. If getting your dog to back up in a straight line is important, you want to practice giving them more space once they consistently back up five to seven steps. Remember to widen their path little by little. Don't take down the cones immediately. Instead, move them over an inch or two each time.

Case Example: Frankie Learns to Back Up

Frankie is a poodle near the end of her adult years. Her owners, Barb and Tony, have become concerned over Frankie when she is in the kitchen. While she has always been in the kitchen when the couple is cooking, Frankie's veterinarian told the couple that she has early stages of arthritis, causing her to walk slower. It's come to the point where the couple almost trip over Frankie in the kitchen because she can't move out of their way quick enough.

After talking to Frankie's previous trainer from her obedience class, they tell Barb to teach Frankie to back up, so she isn't in their way when they are cooking. Barb sets up cones in the middle of the kitchen and focuses on one side to teach Frankie to "back up." Starting at the entrance of the kitchen, Barb takes a few steps into the kitchen. She knows Frankie well enough to know that her dog will follow her.

Once Frankie is near the stove, Barb holds up the treat between her fingertips next to Frankie and starts slowly moving it. Frankie takes a step back, so Barb tosses the treat between her dog's front paws. Frankie takes another couple of steps back, eats the treat, and receives positive reinforcement from Barb.

When Barb tries to get Frankie to back up a little more with another treat, Frankie lays down on the floor and looks up at Barb. Knowing that Frankie is tired, or her joints are starting to bother her, Barb rewards Frankie for her effort and stops training until later.

When Barb tries to train Frankie again, her dog comes into the kitchen, but then immediately lays down. Barb gives Frankie the treat and then comforts her dog as she knows there is something wrong.

After talking to Frankie's veterinarian, Barb learns the best step to take is to train Frankie on carpet or rugs as hard floors are bad for Frankie's joints. Therefore, Barb starts to train Frankie in the living room instead of the kitchen. To ease more on Frankie's joints, Barb only does one round of training twice a day. Within a couple of weeks, Barb has taught Frankie to move backward and out of the kitchen with the verbal cue "back."

Frankie's story gives you an idea of what obstacles training can bring. While Frankie wanted to please her owners, she was also trying to tell Barb that something is wrong by laying on the floor of the kitchen. Hard floors do cause pain for dogs who are showing signs or have arthritis. It is important that you listen to your dog and watch how they are acting during training.

If you feel that something is wrong with your dog, stop training and contact your veterinarian. They will take time to discuss any type of problems and give your dog a check-up to see what they are trying to tell you. While most people think that their dog is going to remain healthy until later in life, many diseases can show themselves in your dog during the adult stage.

Stand on a Platform

If you're training your dog to become a show dog or for agility training, it is important you focus on training your dog to stand on a platform. Of course, you can also train them in this trick for the fun of it. Once your dog stands on the platform, you want to make sure they wait for you to give their next cue. Therefore, if you are doing this for fun, always remember you need to give your dog an ending cue.

Your dog's platform needs to be an elevated flat surface they can jump or climb onto without much trouble. If your dog is having trouble going up and down stairs, you will want to use a ramp to help your dog reach the platform. You can also think of using a specific rug as a platform for senior dogs.

The visual cue for this trick is pointing to the platform. The verbal cue is often "place," "table," or "hup."

1. Get your dog to get to know their platform. Place a few treats around the platform and allow them to sniff the platform, eat the treat, or stand on the platform. The second your dog touches the platform, reward them with verbal praise.

2. Don't start training them to step up on the platform or place your dog on top of the platform. They need to get used to the

platform in their way. This can take a few sessions before they are ready for training.

3. To lure your dog onto the platform, use treat and verbal cues. Hold a treat between your fingertips and start by your dog's face. Slowly move the treat onto the platform. Once they touch the platform, say "place" and give them their treats and positive reinforcement. Mark the place they touched, so you can make sure they go a bit further onto the platform with each session.

4. Once your dog is halfway onto the platform and comfortable with the verbal cue, add in the visual cue. Point to the platform when you say the verbal cue.

5. Once your dog starts to jump onto the platform, toss the treat away from the platform. Repeat this process for a few seconds.

6. When your dog starts following your verbal and visual cues, slowly decrease luring them with a treat.

7. When your dog stays on the platform for a few seconds, tell them to "sit." Once they sit for a few seconds, toss the treat.

8. Move the platform around your home so they become familiar with the trick and not the location. This is necessary for show dogs as they will be in different areas when needing to stand on a platform.

9. When your dog starts sitting on the platform, take a couple of steps back. The point is to keep your dog on the platform until you give your finishing verbal cue, which can be "down" or "come."

Touching a Target

The target your dog will touch with their nose is any type of flat and safe target. You can use a target, round lids, sticky notes, paper, or squares from the carpet. You want the target to be medium sized and something that your dog won't associate with a toy. You can also train your dog to touch the target with their paw.

The visual cue you will use is pointing to the target. If you decide to train your dog to touch the target with their nose and paw, you want to create two types of visual cues. For instance, you could point to the target with your finger for nose touching and point to the target with your hand held out and your palm aimed at your dog for paw touching.

The verbal cue you will use for targeting is "target." Again, if you are training your dog for nose and paw touching, you will want two verbal cues. For example, you can use "target" for nose touching and "touch" for paw touching.

1. Decide if you will teach paw or nose touching first, or only one.

2. Choose a target that will interest your dog, but not to the point they will want to play with the target. You want them to focus on the target.

3. Test your dog's interest with the target by tossing the target on the floor. Make sure you have your dog's attention.

4. If your dog looks at the target, give them positive reinforcement.

5. Leave the target on the floor and encourage your dog to walk close to the target. After they take a few steps or walk to the target, give them positive reinforcement.

6. When your dog touches the target for the first time, give them more positive reinforcement than the last few steps. You might do this by playing with them for a few seconds

with their favorite toy or giving them a treat. Focus on this step for a few sessions.

7. Now, limit your dog's positive reinforcement for touching the target with their nose or paw. Remember to just focus on one. For example, your dog touches the target with their nose, so you say the verbal cue "target" and reward them. Focus on this step for a few sessions.

8. With the target in a certain spot and your dog a few inches away, say "target," and point to the target. When your dog touches the target with their nose, give them positive reinforcement. If your dog doesn't move to the target easily, reward your dog each time they move a bit closer to the target.

9. Once your dog is touching the target with their nose after your cues, start moving the target around the house and continue to practice.

Case Example: Minnie and Her Target

Minnie loves to learn new tricks. As a way to keep her older dog's mind active, Minnie's companion, Trisha, found the "target" trick. After reading the steps, she decides that her dog can easily learn how to touch a target with her nose. For the target, Trisha uses a yogurt lid.

In her dog's sleeping area, Trisha tosses the lid onto the floor. Minnie, who was playing with a toy, looks at the lid and quickly becomes curious about what just fell in her sleeping area. Slowly, Minnie gets up to sniff the new lid. Trisha rewards her dog with positive reinforcement and a treat.

For the next session, Trisha moves the target to a specific location in Minnie's sleeping area. With Minnie across the room, Trisha says "Minnie" to get her attention. When Minnie looks, Trisha waves to motion Minnie to "come." Minnie follows the command and Trisha rewards her dog with positive reinforcement.

Trisha then sees Minnie look at the lid, so Trisha says "target" and rewards Minnie with a treat. When Minnie takes a step toward the lid, Trisha responds with "target" and gives Minnie another treat. Each time Minnie takes a couple of steps closer to the target, Trisha gives Minnie positive reinforcement.

Once Trisha says "target" and Minnie responds by going to the target, Trisha starts using the visual cue of pointing. After following his for a couple of sessions, Trisha focuses on getting Minnie to touch the target with her nose. Trisha says "Minnie, target" and points to the target. Whenever Minnie touches the target with her nose, Trisha rewards Minnie with positive reinforcement. Over a few sessions, Minnie always responds by touching the target with her nose.

Cleaning Up Toys

No matter what age a dog is, they can leave a mess with their toys. As long as your dog understands fetch and that their toys go into a box, they can clean up their toys with a little encouragement.

If your dog's toys aren't already in a specific box, place them in a box that can store all of your dog's toys. Let this box full of toys that sit in your dog's sleeping area for a while and take out toys to play with. This will get them used to the fact that their toys are in this box. Remember, clean up your dog's toys at least once a day so they have to retrieve their toys from the box over and over.

The visual cue will be pointing to the toy box. The verbal cue will be "clean" or "clean up." You can also use "pick up."

1. When you start training your dog to pick up their toys, take all the toys out of the box and place one in the box. Ask your dog to fetch the toy. If they are confused, walk them to the box and ask them to fetch. Once your dog picks up the toy, set your hand on the box and ask your dog to give the toy to you.

You may need to use the phrase "drop" like you do during fetch. When they drop the toy, place it into the box and reward your dog. When you reward your dog, give them a treat by holding it over the box.

2. Teach your dog to drop the toy in the box. Once your dog has the toy in their mouth, point to the box. If they drop the toy outside of the box, give your dog attention for trying. If your dog drops the toy inside the box, give them a treat and attention.

3. Take the toy out of the box and ask them to fetch it to practice dropping the toy in the box.

4. Once your dog is dropping one toy in the box continuously, add another toy.

5. Include the verbal cue with your visual cue. Point the box and say, "fetch, clean up." When your dog picks up the toys and places them in the box, reward them with a treat and attention. If they don't drop them inside the box, give them attention for their effort.

6. Once your dog is cleaning up two toys, add in more toys.

7. When your dog is consistently placing the toys in the box, drop the "fetch" and just say "clean up."

Catch a Ball

To catch a ball, it is best to teach your dog to fetch and play tug and release first. These are often known as building blocks to a game of catch. The point of this game is for you to toss a toy, such as a ball, into the air and your dog catches it in their mouth.
It's important to note that not all dogs like to play catch. If you find that your dog tends to move away when you toss an object instead of trying to catch it, they might be too afraid to catch an object in their mouth. Don't force your dog to learn catch.

For this trick, you want two identical balls. Practice tossing the balls gently before introducing the balls to your dog. The verbal cue for this trick is "catch."

1. Introduce one ball to your dog by rolling it on the floor by them. Keep the other ball in your hand. Your dog is going to become interested in the ball rolling their way. As the ball is rolling, you can build your dog's drive to get the ball by saying "get" just as you would during fetch. Once your dog is playing with the ball, give them positive reinforcement.

2. Take the ball your dog is playing with and hold it up to them. Toss it to them gently and say "catch." You want to toss it gently toward their mouth. The more the ball ends at your dog's mouth, the more confident they will feel about catching the ball. When your dog catches the ball in their mouth, give them positive reinforcement and a treat. If they let the ball drop to the floor without catching, give them positive reinforcement for effort.

3. Once your dog catches the ball a few times in their mouth, ask them to "give" the ball back to you. This is when the second ball comes in handy. The second your dog drops the ball from their mouth, give them positive reinforcement and gently toss the other ball in their direction.

4. Once your dog is trying to catch the ball confidently, start backing up by taking a step each time you toss the ball.

Chapter 6

Tips and Tricks for Training Your Senior Dog

Depending on your dog's breed, the senior age will start between six to ten years of age. If you just brought home your dog, you will want them to get used to the environment before you look at training. Instead of letting your dog take a week to get comfortable, give them a couple of weeks. You always want to allow a senior dog more time because they are starting to slow down in general.

Furthermore, you never know the background of your dog. If they are older and come from a shelter, they could have a lot of traumatic experiences in the back of their mind. This means they will need more time to get used to their new environment and become comfortable around their new family.

People often feel that you need to have more patience bringing home a senior dog than you do with a puppy. The main reason for this is because puppies adjust quickly since everything is new and exciting for them. When it comes to a senior dog, changes can cause a lot of anxiety and be overwhelming.

This can also cause them to have frequent accidents, even if they are potty trained. Don't become frustrated or angry with your dog if they have accidents. Understand that it is part of their system when things are changing, and they are feeling overwhelmed. Comfort your dog and let them know that you love them.

Keeping a Senior Dog Healthy

You are going to spend more time worrying about the health of your old dog than you are at any other age. Many people feel that a senior dog should see the veterinarian at least four times a year. If they start to have health problems, this can increase. Here are some other tips to follow when it comes to keeping your older dog healthy:

Pay Close Attention to Their Diet

You always want to pay attention to your dog's diet. You want to purchase nutritious food for their age that gives them all the nutrients they need. However, this becomes more important as your dog age and lifestyle. Senior dogs will benefit from a diet that has fewer calories and less fat.
You want to focus on vitamins and other minerals. This changes because senior dogs are less active than younger dogs. It's also important to make sure there is fiber in your dog's diet because senior dogs are more prone to constipation. Many people like to feed their senior dog some fruits and vegetables instead of just hard or soft dog food.

Dental Hygiene

Senior dogs can easily start to lose their teeth. It is important that you take your dog in for teeth cleanings, which is something that your veterinarian can do. Keep up with a check-up every six months and inspect your dog's teeth and gums at least once a week.
If you notice something doesn't look right or your dog has a loose tooth, call your veterinarian immediately. This can cause your dog pain. Furthermore, your dog can get food stuck in the hole in their gums and this can lead to an infection.

Make Sure Your Dog Gets Exercise

Your older dog is not going to pay as much attention to exercise. You might find your dog, especially if they are not doing well, not wanting to exercise. Do your best to get your dog up and walking. A larger dog's exercise should go beyond a walk around the block or take them around the block a couple of times a day. However, your smaller dog might feel like a walk around the block is a bit too much.
If you just brought home your dog and you are not sure if they are used to exercise, you want to start slow and gradually increase the amount of exercise they get in one day. Remember to notice how they handle hotter days. If your dog can't be outside for long on a hot day, make sure they get more exercise indoors. Walk them around the house or play with them more.

Provide Your Dog with Special Accommodations

Your older dog will have health issues. One of the most common problems for older dogs is arthritis. This is a painful disease and you want to do more than give your dog medication to help ease their discomfort. For example, dogs with arthritis benefit from towels, blankets, and other soft bedding. If you have stairs they need to climb, think of installing a ramp for them. Any hard floors that they need to walk on should have some type of rugs or carpeting for them.

Training Techniques for Senior Dogs

The most important factor to keep in mind with your senior dog is how much they can handle. There are tricks that you won't want to teach your older dog, such as agility training, hunting, or any tricks that can cause them to become tired quickly or hurt themselves. For example, if your dog doesn't climb stairs well, you will want to keep this in mind when training.

Senior dogs can learn the basic tricks, such as home base, sitting, and lying down without too much trouble. While you can usually train them for about ten minutes at a time, if you feel your dog is becoming tired or it's a hot day, you need to shorten the time and allow them to relax.

If you would like professional help with training your senior dog, think about enrolling them in obedience classes. Obedience classes do not have age limits. Any breed of any age can start learning tricks through these classes.

Training Tips for Senior Dogs

The training tips for older dogs discussed in the previous chapter need to be kept in mind when you are training your senior dog. At the same time, these dogs are near the end of their life and require extra attention when training. Here are some other tips to keep in mind.

Watch the Repetition

When you are teaching a younger dog tricks, you are told that repetition is key. This is something you don't want to do with senior dogs because of their joints. Repetition will cause any arthritis to flare up. It can also cause flare ups even if they don't show any signs of arthritis yet. This means you won't want to make your senior dog sit seven times in a row. Instead, have them sit a couple of times, or once if it makes you feel more comfortable, and then give them a bit of a break.

If you are training your dog to sit or lay down and they don't want to respond, don't get frustrated. The trick might cause them discomfort of pain. Instead, stop worrying about training, make your dog comfortable, and get them into the veterinarian for a checkup.

Shorten the Training Time

It's fine to train older dogs for then minutes at the time, but your senior dog may not handle this amount of time too well. If you start to notice your dog becoming tired or uninterested in training, start shortening the training time. Observe your dog during training and pay attention to when they start to get more sluggish and tired. If it is about four minutes into training, focus on training for only a couple of minutes.

Use Verbal Cues and Hand Gestures to Train Your Senior Dog

It's fine to use an e-collar or clicker for training a younger dog, but to train your older dog, you should stick to training signals, or verbal cues or hand gestures. If your dog is going blind, use verbal cues, and if they are going deaf, use hand gestures. Even if you used an e-collar when your dog was younger, the shock can cause them to move quickly or in a way that can cause more pain in the joints.

Train Your Dog on Soft Surfaces

Because of your dog's arthritis, it is best to train your dog on carpet, rugs, or other soft surfaces. Furthermore, training on a soft surface is more comfortable for your dog's paws and bones.

Which Hand?

The tricks in this chapter can be taught to your dog sooner. These tricks are ones that are easy to grasp and don't require a lot of time from your older dog. However, you should only focus on teaching your senior dog new tricks if they are capable of accomplishing them. If you start training your dog and find that they become tired or stop focusing on the step and lay down, your dog is telling you that it's not time to learn this trick. While you want to keep your dog's mind going throughout their life, it is important you don't push your dog to take on a trick that they don't feel like doing.

Which hand is a simple trick that most dogs enjoy because they focus on picking the hand with the treat in it. The challenge is you want your dog to place their paw up on your hand, telling you which hand they pick.

This trick is often used for police and military dogs because it focuses on a dog's scent. It will help them build up their scent skills by focusing on the area the scent is coming from.

At the beginning, your dog might need a little hint to let them know which hand the treat is in. At the same time, if your dog is losing their smell, you will want to give them a little hint to show them which hand the treat is in. You can do this by gently shaking your hand a bit.

1. Get down to your dog's eye level and place a treat in your hand. Show your dog the treat.

2. Close your hand to make a fist.

3. Ask your dog "which hand?" and command your dog to sit. Your dog should sit facing the hand with the treat.

4. Open your hand with the treat and allow your dog to eat the treat. Don't use the same hand each time. You want to switch it up, but make sure that they see which hand the treat is in to start.

5. After a few successful sessions, stop cueing your dog to "sit" and just ask "which hand?" Your dog should sit without being told to with the cue of "which hand?"

6. With a treat in your hand, stand in front of your dog.

7. With your dog looking at your hands, switch the treat from one hand to the other. Allow your dog to watch you make a fist to hide the treat.

8. Say "which hand?" Remember to make sure your hands are not close together so your dog can easily let you know which hand the treat is in.

9. Once your dog successfully choses the correct hand, place both hands behind your back and show your dog two fists. Place your fists close to your dog's nose.

10. Say "which hand?" If your dog chooses the correct hand, allow them to eat the treat. If they chose the wrong hand, open the hand with the treat in it. Don't say or do anything as you want your dog to notice the treat is in the other hand. Don't let her take the treat. Instead, close your hand to make a fist and ask your dog "which hand?" Repeat this until your dog picks the right hand.

Case Example: Prince Picks a Hand

Prince is a senior dog who used to be highly active. He took part in dog sports and even won a few awards. Unfortunately, over the last couple of years, Prince has struggled with arthritis and is losing his hearing. Because of this, Prince can't take part in a lot of the tricks he loved to do.

Since Prince can't do much, his companion, Denise, has looked at different tricks to teach her dog. She knows that one of the best ways to keep Prince happy is to keep his mind active.

While Prince is laying beside the couch one day, Denise sits down by him with a treat. Prince watches as Denise places the treat in her right hand. She shows Prince the treat and then makes two fists. Knowing that Prince won't hear her well, she gently shakes her right hand. Prince bumps her right hand with his nose, causing Denise to open up her hand and allows Prince to eat the treat. Because of Prince's age and declining health, Denise only repeats this trick twice during a session. They have four training sessions a day.

Within the week, Denise places the treat in her hand before she sits down by Prince. While Prince does not see the treat, he knows one hand has the treat. He waits for Denise's little shake of a hand to pick which hand. At this time, Denise doesn't shake right away because she is trying to get Prince to smell the treat in her hand instead.

One day, during the second week of this training, Denise sits down and within a few seconds, Prince bumps his nose on her left hand. Smiling, Denise opens her hand to show Prince that he picked the correct hand. While Prince doesn't always get the correct hand, he is starting to understand he needs to sniff both hands and one will have a stronger treat smell than the other.

The story of Prince and Denise shows that it's perfectly fine to change the steps of a trick, as long as you don't lose sight of the point for the trick. Denise had the goal that Prince would pick the hand which held the treat through smell. Because he doesn't hear well, she knew that using verbal cues would not help. Therefore, she used a visual cue to help Prince learn the trick.

Chapter 7

So, You Want to Train Your Dog to Dance and Other Tricks

Keeping Your Dog Active

The reason people continue to train their dog, no matter what age, is because it helps keep their dog active. You want to keep your dog as active as possible, without causing them to become too tired or stressed, physically and mentally. There might be times where your dog can't do certain tricks anymore. If this happens, try to find a new trick to teach your dog that will be appropriate for their age and ability level.

Fortunately, for those long winter days or dogs that can't handle a lot of tricks, there are other ways to keep your dog healthy and active.

- Have them find treats around a room. Don't spread the treats everywhere unless your dog can handle spending a lot of time on their paws.

- Walk around the house with your dog.

- Play inside games, such as tug and release.

- Purchase toys that you can place food and treats inside. Give them to your dog and let them play and work for their treats.

- Hide your dog's toys and tell them to find their toys. You will want to give their toys names and teach them these names before you play this game.

- Practice tricks they know and can perform.

Always Remember Safety

One of the biggest reasons you will teach your dog basic tricks is because it will help keep them safe. For example, you can teach your dog to sit and stay if you are near a road, so they don't run after a car or a dog they find interesting. You will teach them "get down" so they don't hurt someone by jumping on them or don't climb up on something they can fall off.
You always want to keep in mind what your dog can and can't handle when you are training. If you try to train your dog to learn a trick and you find them struggling too much, you may need to focus on an easier trick.
With over a hundred tricks that your dog can learn, it's impossible to get them all in this book. However, I wanted to focus on different tricks because each dog breed will be different when it comes to learning tricks. Some dog breeds will strive on agility training while other dogs are more interested in hunting. If your get a dog from a shelter who is older, there are several tricks you can't teach your dog because of their health and age. But you can always teach dogs the basic tricks and then branch out into some of the easier tricks.
The tricks in this chapter are going to focus on basic, intermediate, and advanced tricks. Remember, you want to start basic, but how quickly your dog advances with the level of tricks they learn depends on their personality and your consistency, not their age.

Traditional Favorites

Sit Pretty

The trick to sit pretty is also known as beg. This is a trick a younger dog will do as it involves the dog sitting on their back paws and holding up their front paws in the air. Dogs who are older may have a problem with this trick because it will put too much pressure on the joints of their back legs, which is bad for arthritis.

The verbal cue for this trick is the word "beg." The visual cue is you placing both your hand up by your chest and holding your fingers down.

1. Command your dog to come to you. Praise them for listening to the command.

2. Tell your dog to sit.

3. When they are sitting, use a treat to lure your dog's head up and back. At the same time, you want to say, "beg." Don't drop the treat into your dog's mouth or beside your dog. Let your dog nibble the treat from your fingertips. This will help your dog stay in the position longer.

    At this point, you don't want your dog's front paws to lift up off the floor. If they do, the treat is too high for them to reach and you should lower the treat for them.

4. Repeat this trick for a few sessions until you notice your dog holding better balance.

5. With the treat in your fingertips, repeat the same process, but raise the treat a little bit so your dog has to stand on their back legs. Again, let your dog nibble on the treat so they can work on their balance. If you have a larger dog, stand behind your dog and move the treat from the front of their face back toward you.

Don't go so far that your dog decides to turn around. You want your dog to work on standing with their two back legs. It might help your larger dog to lean against you and you hold their chest to keep them in the position at first. Soon, they will be strong enough to handle the position themselves.
6. When your dog's balance starts to improve, move away and place your hands in the visual cue position and say "beg." Toss the treat to your dog. The key is to toss the treat when your dog is still standing in the right position.

Speak

If you are trying to train your dog not to bark but becoming frustrated because they don't listen, you may want to try this trick. Speak allows your dog to bark on cue instead of at whatever causes them to bark. The verbal cue for this trick is "speak" or "bark." The visual cue is holding your hand in the "L" shape.

1. Before you start training your dog to speak, you want to take time to observe your dog. What makes your dog bark? Is it the mailman, a doorbell, or seeing you drive up the driveway? You will want to pick one factor that makes your dog bark as stimulus for the training. For the purpose of this trick, I am going to use the sound of a doorbell.

2. Standing in front of your door, say "bark" and ring the doorbell. When your dog barks, reward them with positive reinforcement. Repeat this step a few times before you move on to the next step, which needs to be in the same session.

3. Stop ringing the doorbell and tell your dog, "bark." If your dog barks, give them a treat. If they don't bark after a few times, go back to the previous step.

4. Once your dog barks when you tell them to, but not when they hear the doorbell, go into a different room. Tell your

dog to "bark." If they are hesitant or don't bark after a few times, return to the front door to practice some more.

Shake Hands

When your dog learns to shake hands, they will raise their paw to their chest height. Anyone who wants to shake your dog's paw will need to from this height. It is important that you don't force your dog to perform this trick if they are showing signs of fear. Many dogs become fearful around strangers or in a room with a lot of people. You want your dog to shake hands with people they are comfortable with.

The verbal cue for this trick is "shake." If you want to teach your dog to shake hands with both paws, you will have "shake" for one paw and "paw" for the other paw. The visual cue to use is holding up to fingers. If you do this visual cue for a different trick, you can point the two fingers down or in a certain direction.

1. Command your dog to sit in front of you. Praise them for listening to your command.

2. With a treat hiding in your right hand, place it low to the ground so your dog can easily touch your hand.

3. Encourage your dog to paw at your hand by saying "get." When your dog lifts up their left paw, give them a treat. When your dog starts to raise their left paw when your hold out your hand, change "get" to "shake."

4. Lift up your hand a bit and say "shake." Once your dog lifts their left paw up to their chest, reward them.

5. Once your dog catches on to the verbal cue and raises their paw to their chest, start using the visual cue with the verbal cue. Eventually, you will stop using the verbal cue and stick with the visual cue.

Silly Dog Tricks

Act Ashamed

Act ashamed is an advanced dog trick that people love to teach their dog because it looks cute. Most people don't teach their dog this trick. However, many dogs start doing this when they do something you don't approve of because they are ashamed. Your dog is smart, and they will quickly catch onto the meaning of this trick.
Most people use the verbal cue of "shame." However, you can use a more positive word if you want to make sure this trick stays silly for your dog. The visual cue is often one finger held up.
1. Use a cushion that is affixed to the back of a chair. Show your dog that you have a treat in your hand. Place the treat under the cushion, but in the front so it is easy for your dog to get to. Tell your dog to "get" to encourage them to go for the treat.

2. Over time, you will place the treat further under the cushion, causing them to bury their heads into the cushion to look for the treat. After a few times, say "shame" when your dog buries their head under the cushion to look for the treat.

3. Slowly, you will stop using the treat and tell your dog "shame," which gives them the cue to look under the cushion for a treat.

4. From the back of the chair, reach into where your dog's mouth is and place a treat near it, allowing them to grab the treat.

5. After a few times, hold the treat in your fist. When you notice them smelling your hand for their treat, tell them to "wait" and release the treat in a couple of seconds.

Expert Tricks

Find the Car Keys or Remote

It happens to everyone: We all lose track of our car keys. We often wish that we could tell our dog to help us look for our keys. Well, there is a trick to teach your dog to help find your car keys or remote.
If you train your dog to find both the car keys and remote, you will have two verbal cues. You will either say, "keys, find it" or "remove, find it."

1. Fill a small key chain bag with a few treats and attach it to your car keys.

2. Toss the keys in a playful manner and tell your dog "keys, fetch." When your dog brings the keys back to you, open the bag and give your dog one of the treats. Your dog will know there are treats in the bag before they bring it back to you. Because they can't open the bag without bringing it back to you, they will quickly learn to bring you the keys. If they do try to open the bag instead of brining you treats, this is usually the case when it comes to puppies, gently take the keys from them and try again.

3. After a few successful sessions, cue your dog by saying, "keys, find it," instead of "keys, fetch."

4. Once your dog constantly brings your keys back to you, hide them in a room.

5. Command your dog to come to you.

6. Say, "keys, find it," and help your dog search the room. Allow your dog to find the keys so they bring them to you. Reward your dog with a treat and praise.

Get the Mail

Most dogs love to have anything to do with the mail. Your dog may have a connection with your mailman, they may enjoy playing with the newspaper or have made a mess of your mail trying to grab it. You can teach your dog to bring the mail to you without ruining any of your bills.

The verbal cue for this trick can be different phrases as it depends on who the dog is bringing the mail to and where. For the purpose of this trick, I am going to use "bring to the table" because the dog is to place the mail on a little table by the door. This cue won't work if a table is too tall for your dog. You can always ask them to bring it to you, someone else, or train them to set it down somewhere.

1. Place an envelope, some mail, or a piece of paper where the mail drops at your door.

2. Stand by the table you want your dog to place the mail at with a few treats.

3. Command your dog to "come" and praise them when they do.

4. Walk your dog to the mail and tell them to "take it." To help them understand, you can point to the mail. Because this is more of an advanced trick, your dog may understand you with the phrase "take it" or your pointing. If they don't, place the mail into their mouth and help them set it on the table.

5. If your dog grabs the mail themselves, point to the table and say "drop" once your dog is close enough to the table. Reward your dog and repeat the process.

6. Every time the mail comes, meet your dog at the door, so you can give them their commands.

7. Once your dog understands to grab the mail, change the verbal cue to "bring to table" instead of "drop." Over time,

your dog will automatically bring the mail to the table and you won't have to use your verbal cues. However, you will want to ensure that your dog is doing their job. If they need reminders, use the verbal cues and give them praise when they follow through.

Dancing

You should only teach any type of dancing or sports tricks to dogs who are really active. If you have an older dog, you can teach them some dance moves, but you will want to make sure they have a strong grasp of training and repetition won't bother their joints or cause them pain.

Heel Forward and Backward

The two cues for this trick are "heel" and "back." The visual cue is to make a fist and place it on the side of your stomach. The dog will always walk on your left side when they are doing heel walks. Your dog should also sit when you stop.

1. To help guide your dog, you may want to place them on a loose leash and set them on your left side.

2. Say "heel" and walk forward with your left foot first. Your left foot will soon become your dog's signal to heel.

3. Each time your dog completes a heel command, praise them with positive reinforcement.

4. When you stop, start to slow your walking. Place your left foot flat on the floor. With your right foot, hold it up in the air and set it right beside your left foot. Command your dog to sit. Reward your dog with positive reinforcement once they sit. The cue for your dog to sit will become your right

leg going up and then landing next to your left foot. Your dog will also learn that this cue is soon coming because you slow down your walking pace.

5. To have your dog walk back, say "back" and take a step back. If your dog doesn't motion, move them with the leash or guide them to take a step back. Once they move, reward them with positive reinforcement.

Take a Bow

Teaching your dog to take a bow is relatively easy and can be done during the basic training stage. The verbal cue is "bow" and your visual cue is placing one foot behind your other foot. The foot that is behind you should rest on tiptoes, just as your feet would do if you bow or curtsy.
When your dog bows, the position they stand in is keeping their legs upright and placing their front leg's elbows on the floor.

1. Command your dog to come to you. Praise them for listening.

2. With your dog facing you, have them stand.

3. Place a treat in your fist and hold it at the nose.

4. Gently, place your hand on your dog's nose and press downward. Give the cue of "bow."

5. When your dog's elbows touch the floor, release the treat.

If your dog doesn't bow down easily, you may need to break the trick down in steps. For example, give your dog the treat when they start to bend their front legs or place their head down.

Chapter 8

Common Mistakes

It's going to happen no matter how hard you try to make your dog's training journey as pleasant as possible—you will make a mistake. You will make several mistakes. However, you and your dog will often make mistakes together. When you start to train your dog, it is a lifelong commitment for your dog, and you need to be as consistent as possible for your dog to thrive through their training journey. It doesn't matter what trick they are learning or what they already know; consistency is one of the biggest keys to successful training.

However, you should never get frustrated when you or your dog makes a mistake in training. You always want to have the mindset that mistakes happen. Learn from your mistake and move on. Don't dwell on your mistakes and don't react harshly toward your dog when they make a mistake. Always remember that your dog is learning just as you are.

One way to keep yourself from limiting the number of mistakes made in the training journey is learning about the common mistakes and keeping them in mind. When you notice that you are on your way to making a mistake, you will be mindful enough to recognize it and stop yourself from making this mistake. If you do make a mistake, you are mindful enough to realize it, learn from it, and move on.

Mistake #1: Training Your Dog for Too Long

You always want to keep in mind that your dog can only train for a specific period of time before it starts to become boring, too stressful, or they become too distracted.

Dogs, no matter what age, don't have a long attention span and they can't focus on one task for several minutes at a time. A puppy's training session should only be a couple of minutes. Of course, obedience classes will go for a longer period of time, but this doesn't mean you should do this at home.

Obedience classes are run in a certain way by professional dog trainers. Allow them to handle the longer training sessions. You can start to train an adolescent dog for about a minute or two longer. An adult dog has an attention span that can last up to six or seven minutes. Senior dogs, unless they have health issues, can last about eight to ten minutes.

Just because you need to limit the amount of time, doesn't mean you can only train once a day. You can hold several training sessions throughout the day for your younger dogs. Your older dogs, especially senior dogs, should be limited to what they can handle. You will learn what your dog can and can't handle by observing your dog.

Some people will use a timer to help them stay within the training limit they set for their dog. People also schedule training sessions every couple of hours for younger dogs and two to three times a day for older dogs.

Mistake #2: You Lack Consistency

Remaining consistent is the main problem people have when it comes to training. However, it is a key when it comes to training your dog in any trick. Even when your dog comes to learn the trick confidently and tends to follow the trick automatically, you still want to make sure that you don't miss a step or don't forget to give them the cues you need to.

One of the hardest parts is correcting your dog's behavior when it comes to training. Many people will use the e-collar to correct their dog's behavior through tricks. However, if their dog does something they aren't supposed to do and the owner doesn't have their remote to give their dog a signal handy, they are going to miss the opportunity. If you decide to keep your dog's e-collar on throughout the day (they should never wear it when they are sleeping), you want to keep the remote with you throughout the day. You can always purchase a smaller remote that can clip on your belt or fit easily into your pocket.

You always need to remember, whether it comes to correcting your dog's behavior or rewarding the behavior, it has to occur within a few seconds from the behavior. For example, if you are teaching your dog not to dig in the garbage behind the garage with the e-collar, you want to send your dog the signals while they are digging. If you do this after or before they can associate the signal to what they are seeing or doing at that time. If you want to praise your dog because they picked up their toys without you commanding them to, you want to do this right after they pick up their toys or they won't understand why they are being praised.

Mistake #3: You Wait Too Long to Start Training

While you don't want to start training your dog the second they walk through your dog, you do want to start within the first week or two, no matter how old your dog is. Even if you brought home a senior dog, start training them the basics. If they know the basics, they will quickly catch onto your cues or simply act on the trick when you give the cue. This often happens when it comes to "sit" because this is the common cue for the command.

You also want to remember that the same day you bring your dog home, you will start training them, it is just not through sessions. For example, you will show them where they will eat, use the bathroom, and sleep. Always remember, whenever you teach your dog something new, it is training.

Mistake #4: You Use Harsh Discipline

Training is a form of discipline as it helps your dog understand how they should act and often corrects their behavior. There is no need to ever hit, kick, or even place your dog in a time out for their behavior. Instead, you want to find a way to train your dog to replace the unwanted behavior with wanted behavior.

This is something that will take time, but your dog is going to trust and respect you more than if you harmed your dog through hitting. Your dog will not become fearful of you, they will learn to listen to your commands and want to do so because they want to make you proud.

Mistake #5: You Stop Training

You should never stop training your dog. Even when your dog is older, you should always practice the tricks they can still complete. For example, if your dog has arthritis, you won't want to focus on agility training, hunting, or dancing. However, they can still sit and lay down. Keep your eye on these tricks as they will help your dog remain active and keep their mind going at the same time.

Your dog will let you know when a trick is becoming too much for their body. You always need to pay attention to your dog's body cues and follow them thoroughly. Your veterinarian and professional dog trainer can also help you understand if you can't read your dog well.

Mistake #6: You Don't Train in the Right Mindset

Training takes a certain mindset. You need to be calm and happy to train your dog, even in the basic training level. Always remember that your dog will feed off your emotions. This means when you are angry, your dog will feel this and cause them to react in fear or become aggressive.

One of the biggest ways to make a dog aggressive is by becoming aggressive toward the dog, including your tone of voice. Dogs are extremely sensitive to voice tones and will quickly pick up on a tone that is not happy or calm.

If you find yourself becoming frustrated or angry during training, or you feel this way before the training session, don't train! It's okay to skip a session or wait until your mood is lighter. Doing this will help the training session go easier and your dog will feel better when they are training.

Mistake #7: Abusing the Training Tools

If you use an e-collar or clicker, be sure that you don't abuse these tools. Some people feel both of these tools need to be used whenever your dog does something you don't want them to do. This is a myth. If you use these tools when you are not training, you will confuse your dog, and this will cause more problems when it comes to training.

More importantly, when it comes to the e-collar, you can harm your dog by sending them signals too often. You won't hurt them physically, unless you don't move the collar around every couple of hours or the collar is on too tightly. You will harm them emotionally and mentally.

Conclusion

There is a lot of information within this book, and while you might feel a little overloaded, as many people do when they read a dog training book, you also feel more confident about training your new family member. Whether you brought home a puppy or an older dog, you have a great amount of information at your fingertips to help you and your dog through the training journey.

You can use this book to help your dog learn tricks from the puppy stage all the way to becoming an adult. At the same time, you can remind yourself of the common mistakes people make so you don't catch yourself doing the same thing. Remember, remaining mindful of your training, supervising your dog, and knowing where any of your training tools will help you stay consistent.

Some of the key takeaways from the contents of this book that you should always remember are:

- Consistency: You always need to be consistent as a dog trainer. Even if you aren't in the mood to get up and praise your dog for exhibiting great behavior, you need to do this. This means it is always helpful to have tools such as treats next to you so you can quickly grab them as a form of positive reinforcement. At the same time, you always need to ensure that you are correcting your dog's unwanted behavior through tricks.

- Always use positive reinforcement: One of the biggest reasons training works so well is because people use positive reinforcement when their dog performs a trick. Some people will even use it when their dog tries but fails or makes a mistake to ensure they keep trying. Dogs thrive on positive reinforcement. They love getting attention from you, so when you are training them, make sure they get as much attention as possible. Positive reinforcement is more than giving your dog a treat!

- Never use harsh discipline: Training your dog is a form of correcting their unwanted behavior and transforming it into wanted behavior. As long as you consistently train your dog and help them through the training process, you will never need to discipline your dog. Instead, you will find a trick that will help your dog learn what to do and what not to do. This means you should never hit, kick, or knee your dog. You never need to perform any type of action that is going to make your dog fear you in any way. The stronger relationship you and your dog have, the better training will go for both of you.

- There is never a perfect time to start training but start after your dog is comfortable: You never want to start demanding your dog to do or act a certain way the minute you walk them through the front door. If they do something they shouldn't, distract them with a toy, but don't give them positive reinforcement. You want your dog to become comfortable with their new environment and the people within it. This includes other pets.

- Always observe your dog's behavior: Your dog will tell you when training is going on for too long. They will tell you when they are not feeling well or are too hot. They will tell you when something is wrong. Even if you are in the middle of training, you have to stop and pay attention to their behavior. If your dog is tired, let them rest. It is more important to keep your dog healthy than making sure they are finishing a certain task.

- Always teach your dog gradually and with small steps: The steps written within the contents of this book are not written in stone. You can break apart the steps to help your dog learn the best way for them. Realize that training is a lifelong commitment for your dog. Once you start, you will train them until they can't take part in the activities anymore. This means you have plenty of time to teach them all the tricks you want to. Go slow and let your dog set the pace. Some dogs will learn faster than other dogs and this is fine. It doesn't mean something is wrong with your dog, it simply means they learn at a slower pace than your friend's dog.

- Have patience: Patience in training is just as important as consistency. You want to train when you are patient and stop when you feel like you are losing your patience.

- Never train when you are angry: Training when you are angry is one of the top ways to teach a dog to become aggressive. Your dog will associate the feelings they get from you to their training. Furthermore, if you are angry your dog might think that they did something wrong when you are angry about a different situation that is completely unrelated to your dog and training. Even if it is time for your dog's at-home training session, don't train if you are angry. You want to wait until you are happy and excited about training as this feeling will be the way your dog feels about training.

- Your dog's mental and emotional health is just as important as their physical health: It is usually easier to understand when something is wrong with your dog physically. It is harder to know if your dog's emotional and mental health is not at a good place, especially if you just brought them home. If you brought home an older dog from the shelter, they could have had traumatic experiences that are still haunting them. Take them to the veterinarian and even a dog behaviorist to make sure everything is good to go before you start training.

- Dental hygiene is important: One factor that many people don't think of is their dog's dental hygiene. However, this is just as important as their physical health. Get treats that will help your dog brush their teeth if they don't allow you to brush their teeth. Make sure your dog has dental check-ups just like they do with physical check-ups.

- Have fun! Even if your dog is learning agility training for dog shows and training is very serious and demanding, you want to make sure that your dog has fun with training. You always want to include play time and make sure they have a period of rest and get enough water, especially on a hot day. Following these tips will help your dog have the best training experience possible.

References

5 Tips for Dog Training Session Prep - Acme Canine. (2017). Retrieved from https://acmecanine.com/5-tips-dog-training-session-prep/

10 Best Training Tips. Retrieved from https://www.pedigree.com/dog-care/training/10-best-training-tips

Becker, M. (2014). The 3 Most Common Dog Training Problems and How to Fix Them. Retrieved from http://www.vetstreet.com/our-pet-experts/the-3-most-common-dog-training-problems-and-how-to-fix-them

Bender, A. (2019). Top 5 Ways to Use Positive Reinforcement to Reward a Dog. Retrieved from https://www.thesprucepets.com/ways-to-reward-a-dog-1118276

Bolluyt, J. (2018). 18 of the Easiest Dog Breeds to Train. Retrieved from https://www.cheatsheet.com/culture/easiest-dog-breeds-to-train.html/

Clark, M. 7 Most Popular Dog Training Methods - Dogtime. Retrieved from https://dogtime.com/reference/dog-training/50743-7-popular-dog-training-methods

Conn, K. (2015). 5 Steps To Correct Inappropriate Dog Chewing. Retrieved from https://www.cesarsway.com/5-steps-to-correct-inappropriate-dog-chewing/

Dog Ages & Stages - Dogtime. Retrieved from https://dogtime.com/dog-health/dog-ages-and-dog-stages/253-ages-stages

Gibeault, S. (2018). 13 of the Most Trainable Breeds. Retrieved from https://www.akc.org/expert-advice/lifestyle/13-of-the-most-trainable-breeds/

Huston, L. Caring for Senior Dogs. Retrieved from https://www.petmd.com/dog/care/evr_dg_caring_for_older_dogs_with_health_problems#

Johnson, D. (2013). Ten Tips for Taking Care of Your Dog. Retrieved from https://iditarod.com/ten-tips-for-taking-care-of-your-dog/

Klinger, C. (2019). When Should I Start Training My Puppy or Kitten? | Hill's Pet. Retrieved from https://www.hillspet.com/pet-care/training/when-to-start-training-puppy-kitten

Lotz, K. Top 10 Senior Dog Training Tips. Retrieved from https://iheartdogs.com/top-10-senior-dog-training-tips/

Obedience Courses. Retrieved from https://www.animalhumanesociety.org/behavior/obedience-courses

Relationship-Based Dog Training: Benefits. Retrieved from https://resources.bestfriends.org/article/relationship-based-dog-training-benefits

Rollins, J. (2016). How to Discipline a Puppy or Dog: Effectively Punishing Your Dog. Retrieved from https://www.petexpertise.com/dog-training-article-using-physical-punishments/

Stages Of Puppy Development. Retrieved from https://dogtime.com/puppies/1130-puppy-behavior-basics-hsus#/slide/1

Tucker, N. (2018). Adolescent Dogs: 6 Facts To Know - Whole Dog Journal. Retrieved from https://www.whole-dog-journal.com/puppies/adolescent-dogs-6-facts-to-know/